T0222856

# Effective Team Management with VSTS and TFS

## A Guide for Scrum Masters

Chaminda Chandrasekara
Sanjaya Yapa

Apress®

*Effective Team Management with VSTS and TFS*

Chaminda Chandrasekara
Dedigamuwa,
Colombo, Sri Lanka

Sanjaya Yapa
Kandy, Sri Lanka

ISBN-13 (pbk): 978-1-4842-3557-7
https://doi.org/10.1007/978-1-4842-3558-4

ISBN-13 (electronic): 978-1-4842-3558-4

Library of Congress Control Number: 2018945102

Managing Director, Apress Media LLC: Welmoed Spahr
Acquisitions Editor: Nikhil Karkal
Development Editor: James Markham
Coordinating Editor: Divya Modi

Cover designed by eStudioCalamar

Cover image designed by Freepik (www.freepik.com)

Distributed to the book trade worldwide by Springer Science+Business Media New York, 233 Spring Street, 6th Floor, New York, NY 10013. Phone 1-800-SPRINGER, fax (201) 348-4505, e-mail orders-ny@springer-sbm.com, or visit www.springeronline.com. Apress Media, LLC is a California LLC and the sole member (owner) is Springer Science + Business Media Finance Inc. (SSBM Finance Inc.). SSBM Finance Inc. is a **Delaware** corporation.

For information on translations, please e-mail rights@apress.com, or visit http://www.apress.com/rights-permissions.

Apress titles may be purchased in bulk for academic, corporate, or promotional use. eBook versions and licenses are also available for most titles. For more information, reference our Print and eBook Bulk Sales web page at http://www.apress.com/bulk-sales.

Any source code or other supplementary material referenced by the author in this book is available to readers on GitHub via the book's product page, located at www.apress.com/978-1-4842-3557-7. For more detailed information, please visit http://www.apress.com/source-code.

Printed on acid-free paper

*Let this book be the ultimate guide for scrum masters to make their team run the extra mile . . .*

# Table of Contents

# About the Authors

**Chaminda Chandrasekara** is a Microsoft Most Valuable Professional (MVP) for Visual Studio Application Lifecycle Management (ALM) and a Scrum Alliance® Certified ScrumMaster (CSM) who believes in continuous improvement of the software development lifecycle. He is a Senior Consultant - DevOps for Tentacle Technologies MSC Sdn.Bhd., Malaysia, assigned to work for Jabil Circuit Sdn. Bhd. He is an active Microsoft Community Contributor (MCC) who is well recognized for his contributions in Microsoft forums, TechNet galleries, wikis, and Stack Overflow and he contributes extensions to Visual Studio Team Services/Team Foundation Server (VSTS/TFS) in the Microsoft Visual Studio Marketplace. He also contributes to other open source projects in GitHub. Chaminda published his first book, *Beginning Build and Release Management with TFS 2017 and VSTS* (www.apress.com/in/book/9781484228104), in June 2017, and he blogs about technology at https://chamindac.blogspot.com and http://devopsbeyondms.blogspot.com/.

## ABOUT THE AUTHORS

 **Sanjaya Yapa** currently works as a Microsoft Dynamics CRM consultant at Oaktan Pty Ltd. in Melbourne, Australia. He has more than 12 years of experience in the industry and has been working with various Microsoft technologies since 2005. Sanjaya possess a wealth of experience in software development, team leadership, product management, and consultancy. He specializes in Microsoft Dynamics CRM and Visual Studio Application Lifecycle Management. Sanjaya blogs on technology and has been sharing his knowledge and expertise via https://techjukebox.wordpress.com and https://almbox.wordpress.com.

# About the Technical Reviewer

**Mittal Mehta** has total 15 years of IT experience. Currently, he is working as a configuration manager and is MCP in TFS 2012. He also has experience working in build-release, DevOps, automation and configuration area since last 8 years in Microsoft Technologies.

# Acknowledgments

A special thank you must go to Indaka Raigama, who has been a brilliant CEO, mentor, and leader for us, and who has given us so many opportunities to research with VSTS/TFS while working for him. It is these opportunities that laid the foundation for this book. Also, we are thankful for all the mentors who have encouraged and helped us during our careers and who have provided us with so many opportunities to gain the maturity and the courage we needed to write this book.

We would also like to thank our friends and colleagues who have helped and encouraged us in so many ways. Last, but in no way least, we owe a huge debt to our families. Not only because they have put up with late-night typing, research, and our permanent air of distraction, but also because they have had the grace to read what we have written. Our heartfelt gratitude is offered to them for helping us make this dream come true.

# Introduction

Agility in software development is becoming mandatory as technology rapidly evolves, causing business processes to improve day by day. Because Visual Studio Team Services/Team Foundation Server (VSTS/TFS) is an application lifecycle management tool, it has enormous capabilities for improving the way a software development team works, if it is used wisely.

The project management role in software development projects/products is now moving toward servant leadership with Agile/Scrum practices, and thus it functions more as a facilitator than as a manager. Tools can help empower teams and enable them to deliver software, with high quality, while rapidly adapting to the changes happening in the tech world. *Effective Team Management with VSTS and TFS: A Guide for Scrum Masters* gives you essential know-how so you can use TFS/VSTS effectively and also enables you to empower your teams. This text provides a deep analysis of practical issues and how to overcome them and details the process of adopting the tool for your style of work.

Rather than just explaining the features, this book describes VSTS/TFS features as solutions to the challenges of building better Agile teams. It also discusses how to handle small, ideally sized Agile teams practically by facilitating large teams to support large-scale projects, by working with distributed teams in different geographical locations, and so on—all skills that deepen your ability to get successful project/product outcomes from your teams. Special focus is given to common pitfalls that you can unintentionally fall into while using the tool that will prevent you from creating teams governed by the terms of the tool, as opposed to teams that find their own better process for creating long-term sustainability.

# CHAPTER 1

# Handling Teams

Agility in software development is becoming mandatory as technology rapidly evolves causing business processes to improve day by day. The project management role in software development projects/products is now moving toward servant leadership with Agile/Scrum practices, thus it functions more as a facilitator and delivery enabler, rather than as a manager. Tools can help empower teams and enable them to deliver software, with high quality, while providing both accountability and visibility. The scrum masters or delivery enablers should use these tools effectively without awakening remnants of the autocratic evil attitude of "I am the project manager, do as I say," which can happen as a result of the overwhelming amount of data and information that is available with a particular tool.

In this chapter, we briefly discuss key concepts of Visual Studio Team Services (VSTS), a cloud version of TFS provided as a software as a service (SaaS), and Team Foundation Server (TFS). Then we dive deep into using VSTS/TFS effectively to overcome the challenges of empowering small, large, and geographically distributed teams.

## VSTS and TFS

Because VSTS/TFS is an application lifecycle management (ALM) tool, it has a wide range of capabilities for improving the ability of a software development team to deliver higher-quality software products/projects in

© Chaminda Chandrasekara, Sanjaya Yapa 2018
C. Chandrasekara and S. Yapa, *Effective Team Management with VSTS and TFS*,
https://doi.org/10.1007/978-1-4842-3558-4_1

a shorter period of time. In this book, you gain essential knowledge and understanding so that you can use VSTS/TFS effectively to empower your teams. The following explanations of VSTS/TFS concepts will help you digest the details we discuss in this and upcoming chapters.

VSTS/TFS offers a collaborative platform on which teams can manage versioning of software code files, plan and track work, including code bugs/defects and issues/impediments they face, and automate the process of building, testing, and releasing software to enable development and operation (DevOps). For further information on key concepts of VSTS/TFS, refer to `https://docs.microsoft.com/en-us/vsts/user-guide/concepts?toc=/vsts/user-guide/toc.json&bc=/vsts/user-guide/breadcrumb/toc.json`.

# Team Project Collections, Team Projects, and Teams

The account in VSTS or a team project collection in on-premises TFS, is the isolated broad grouping of *team projects*. A team project can represent a product/project team or even an entire development team that is working on multiple projects for an organization. In a team project, you are provided with a source control repository (or multiple repositories) and a place in which a team of developers or teams can plan, collaborate, and track the work they are carrying out. Additionally, a team project provides build, test, and deploy components for a software product(s)/project(s). When you create a new team project, a team with a team project name is created by default. You can add more than one team inside your team project.

When you connect to VSTS/TFS, you are connecting with an account or a team project collection. You can define one or more team projects within that collection. When you create a team project, a team by the same name is created by default; this is sufficient for smaller teams.

In a scenario that includes multiple projects and multiple teams, you may need to create multiple team projects and teams under a single account or project collection. For further reading, please refer to `https://docs.microsoft.com/en-us/vsts/user-guide/team-projects-teams-repos#what-is-a-team-project`. We discuss team projects and teams in detail, later in this chapter.

## Work Items

A *work item* is any type of work you do as a team member or as a team. A *work item type (WIT)* in VSTS/TFS is provided with fields, a layout, and a specific workflow that allows you to track the work being carried out by the team. Features, user stories, product backlog items, bugs, tasks, test cases, and so on are some of the available work item types by default. You can also introduce your own work item types and alter the behavior of the existing default work item types. In Chapter 2, we discuss the effective usage of these work items to facilitate your team needs.

## Iterations/Sprints and Areas

You should use the *iteration/sprint* paths to group work into time periods and this is mapping to Agile/Scrum, iterations and sprints concept. You can use the *area* to group the work items for a team, product/project, or feature/module of a piece of software. To learn more details about iterations and areas, refer to `https://docs.microsoft.com/en-us/vsts/work/customize/about-areas-iterations`. We will discuss these in further detail later in this chapter.

Now that you have a basic knowledge of VSTS/TFS concepts, let's focus on the more important aspects of using this tool. Because you are a facilitator (you may be thinking, "Am I not the manager anymore?" The answer is no, you are *not* the manager any longer. Instead, you are the delivery enabler, so change your attitude right *now*!), you may have a few different types of projects/products to deliver with the help of your team(s):

- *Short-Term Project:* This type of project is developed and delivered within a short period of time. Ideally you can handle this project with a small Agile/Scrum team made up of three to nine members as per latest scrum guide.

- *Long-Running or Complex and Large Product/Project:* To deliver this type of project, you will require a large number of team members, and you may have all of them in the same geolocation.

- *Long-Running or Complex and Large Product/Project:* To deliver this type of project, you will require a large number of team members, and you may have them in different geolocations and time zones.

# Determining the Ideal Size for Teams

What is the ideal team size? What you need for a small project that can be completed within three to six months with the short warranty period might differ from what you need for a long-running product that has a roadmap for delivering features in very small chunks, which can be facilitated by a small team. On the other hand you might want to have a large team if it is required to deliver bulk of work urgently, which we will discuss later in this chapter. You may encounter many other project/product requirements that influence team size.

## Getting Started

To begin, it is crucial that you make sure that you are underpinning the right framework for executing the project/product. Let's dive deep into the steps that will help you lay the groundwork for a small team using VSTS/TFS. First you must create the team project for the team.

## Creating a Team Project

Before creating the team project, you need to make the following decisions:

- Determine the process template.

  Out of the box, VSTS/TFS comes with three process templates: Agile, Scrum, and CMMI (Capability Maturity Model Integration). The *process template* defines the work item types and how they behave in your project. Each template has its own pros and cons. Once you have selected the template, it can be customized, but you cannot change it to a different default template at a later stage. So, be sure to discuss this choice with your team and decide which template is best for your project/product development. You can find more information at this link: `https://docs.microsoft.com/en-us/vsts/work/guidance/choose-process`.

- Decide on the version control repository.

  Make sure to consult your technical team before you decide which version control system to use. VSTS/TFS comes with Team Foundation Version Controlling (TFVC) and Git (Team Foundation Git). Each of these repositories has its own advantages and disadvantages. Use this link to help you decide on the best version control system for your situation: `https://docs.microsoft.com/en-us/vsts/tfvc/comparison-git-tfvc`.

Once you have made these two decisions, you can begin creating the team project. To do so, click the gear icon on top right corner of the home page of VSTS/TFS. This action takes you to the Administration Overview page. Click New Team Project to create the new team project.

You can find out more details about creating team projects here: `https://docs.microsoft.com/en-us/vsts/accounts/create-team-project?tabs=vsts`. As illustrated in Figure 1-1, make sure to provide the Project Name, the Version Control, and the Work Item Process template.

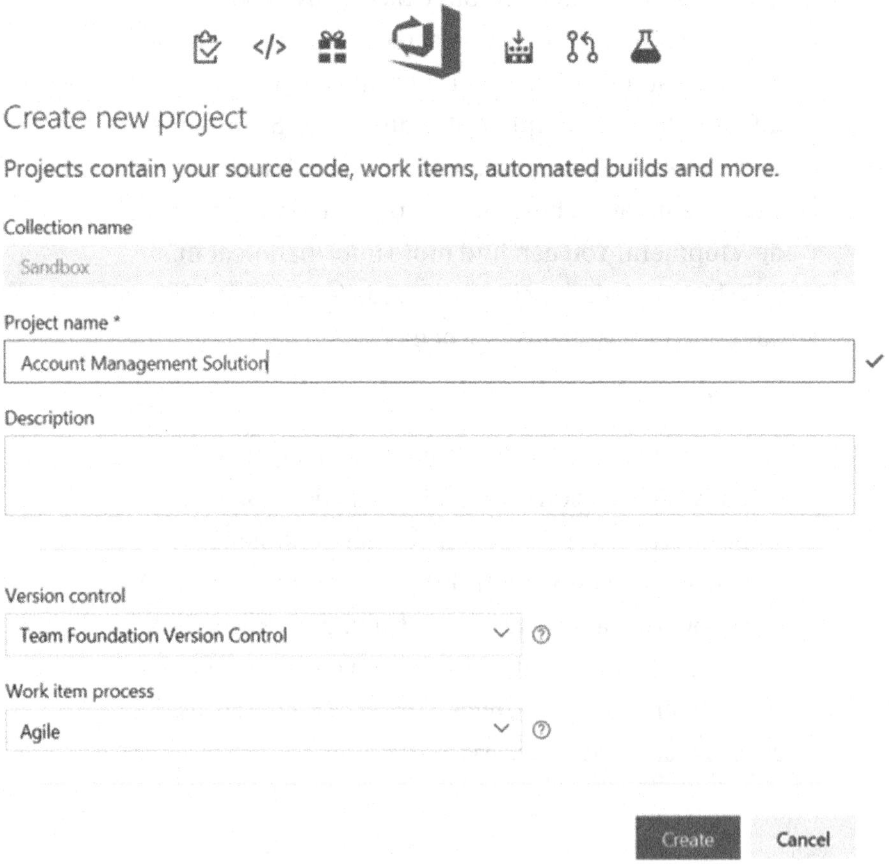

*Figure 1-1.* *Creating a new project*

# Managing Backlog

Regardless of the process model you use, you should have a list of items that you need to complete to deliver a successful project/product. This list of work is made up of product backlog items (PBIs) in Scrum, user stories in Agile, and requirements in CMMI, or, you might even have your own terminology. We discuss backlog management in detail in Chapter 2. Figure 1-2 illustrates a sample backlog.

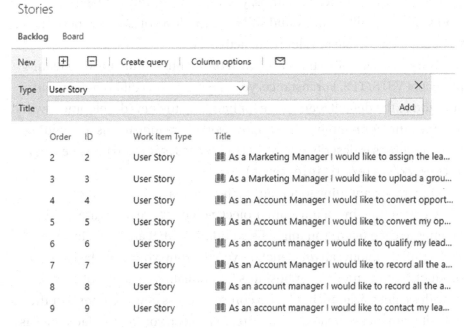

***Figure 1-2.*** *Backlog view*

# Isolating the Work of a Small Team

If you are working on a smaller project and you need to deliver it in a short period of time, you can work with a single team with a backlog. But when the project becomes complex—for instance, if the project needs support once it goes live—how do you handle the complexity of working with new feature development while still supporting production issues?

The challenge here is not to interrupt the ongoing new feature development while you are catering to client issues and fixing them as soon as possible. In such scenarios, you must effectively manage both workloads with full visibility and still require a level of isolation of support work and new feature development activities.

You can accomplish this easily with the Teams feature inside a team project of VSTS/TFS. For instance, you can create two different teams in addition to the default team—one for handling the new development work and the other for handling the support work. (Creating teams and adding team members is described here: `https://docs.microsoft.com/en-us/vsts/work/scale/multiple-teams`).

One important thing to remember here is that, when you create these two new teams in the team project, you must create an area that belongs to each team. You might be wondering what an area is in VSTS/TFS. Fundamentally, an *area* enables you to group your work by its team, product, feature, module, or business functionality. An area not only provides categorization, but it also controls access to work items. For the default team that is created for your team project, you get a default area as well. So, when you create teams, you get the opportunity to select whether the team requires an area or not (see Figure 1-3). To create a new team, follow these steps:

1. Click the Settings(gear) icon on the top right corner of the project portal.

2.  When you are redirected to the Administration page, click the New Team option from the Overview tab.

3.  In the Create New Team page, enter your team name, select your permissions, and make sure the Team Area checkbox is checked. Click Create Team (see Figure 1-3).

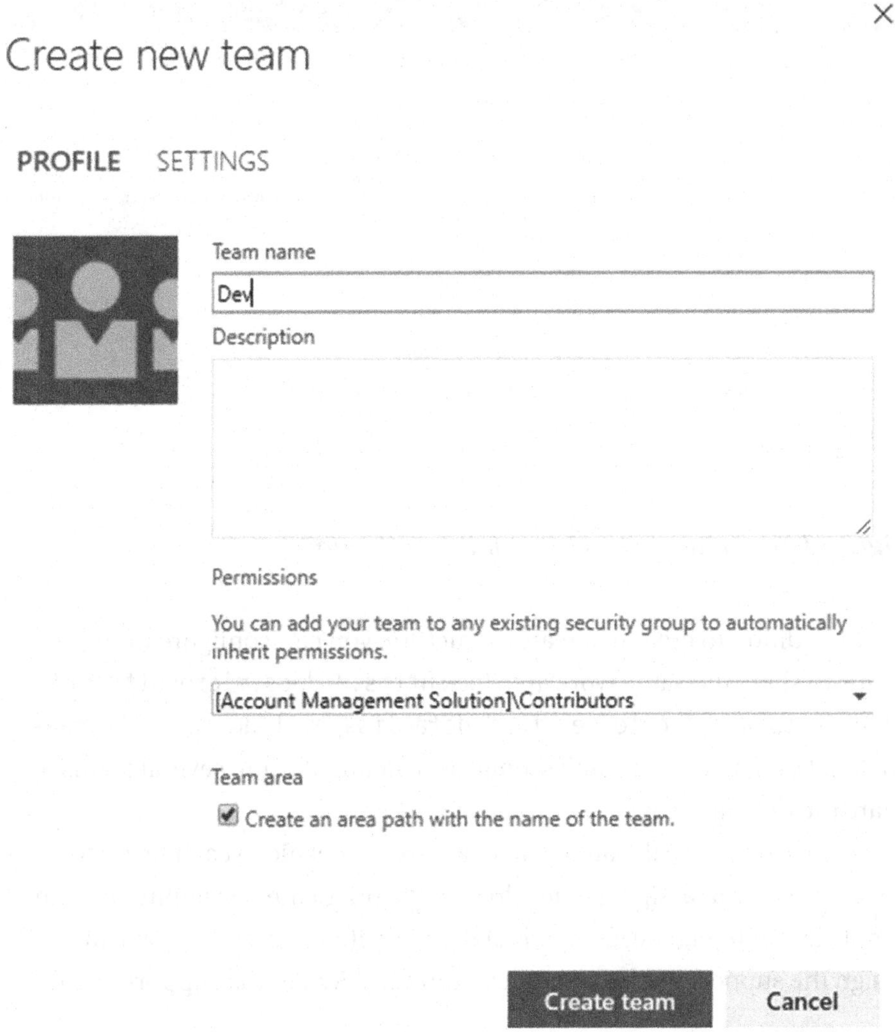

×

# Create new team

**PROFILE**    SETTINGS

Team name

Dev

Description

Permissions

You can add your team to any existing security group to automatically inherit permissions.

[Account Management Solution]\Contributors    ▼

Team area

☑ Create an area path with the name of the team.

Create team    Cancel

*Figure 1-3. Creating a new team*

In Figure 1-4, you must select an area for each team you create so you can organize your backlog and the work items. You can create subareas under each team area, but make sure you do not create an area structure that is too complex; because doing so will cause too much overhead in work item management as well as in permissions management.

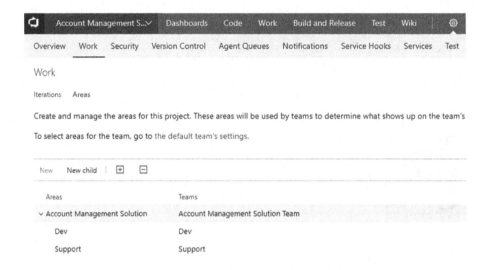

***Figure 1-4.*** *An area structure for a small team*

In addition to creating an area structure, you can configure multiple teams to share the same work area (see `https://docs.microsoft.com/en-us/vsts/work/scale/set-team-defaults#set-team-default-area-paths`). For instance, in some scenarios, you might want, several teams to share the default area.

You can also use the area to allocate work specific to each team; for instance, you can assign the development work to the development team simply by changing the area path of the work item. Similarly, you can assign the support work that comes from the client to the support team by selecting the relevant area, as illustrated in Figure 1-5. The root or default team has visibility across all the teams underneath it when you set it to include subareas for its own area. (Refer to the link in the previous paragraph for more details).

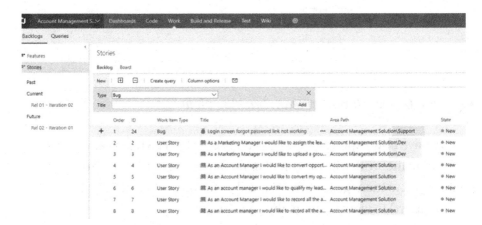

***Figure 1-5.*** *Backlog view from the default/root team*

Work item allocation to the relevant area opens the opportunity to have dedicated backlogs for each team (Figure 1-6). This way, the ongoing development work and the support work does not get mixed up. Further, this also allows team members to work across the teams. In general, a developer may work in both development and support teams, therefore, you can share your team resources (developers and testers) on demand to either of the activities.

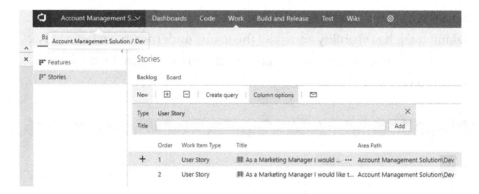

***Figure 1-6.*** *Development team backlog view*

We have now explored how you can use VSTS/TFS teams and areas to separate the work within a small team depending on its activity. This enables you to manage the work as well as for individual action teams (dev/support) to work without any collisions.

## Managing Delivery Cadence

Now that we have set up the teams and the area hierarchy to organize the backlog, it's time to come up with a plan for releasing the goods to the end users. Basically, we need to finalize how often we should do this. We know the clients would love to see the results of their investments as early as possible. In theory, with the Agile practice that we incorporate with the project/ product development work, we should release software to the end users in short iterations. Say you want to have three weeks of iterations; that is, you are planning to release software at the end of every three weeks or your delivery cadence is three weeks. Remember, the software delivery cycle time or delivery cadence might be different based on the complexity of the project.

Once you have decided that the completed work will be released every three weeks (this can be a different time frame such as one week or a month depending on your team needs) or, in other words, that the length of your iterations is three weeks, you can go ahead and set the iterations in VSTS/TFS (Figure 1-7).

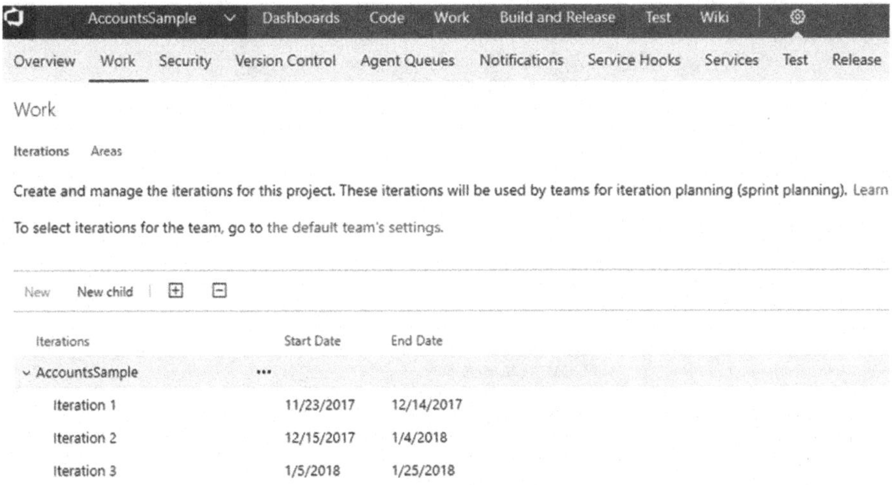

*Figure 1-7.* *Managing iterations*

As mentioned earlier, you can use the areas to organize work items into teams, products, features, modules, or business functionalities, and you can use the iterations to organize your work items based on the release priority. This is where you build your release cadence. So, by the end of each iteration, you and your team will be releasing the software to the end users. But is this actually possible? The reality is that when you kick off the project, by the end of the first iteration of the cycle, most of the time you do not yet have anything to deliver to the users. It might take a minimum of three to four cycles to get something out. What can you do in the meantime to get things lined up nicely?

You can easily set up a release cycle with a release hierarchy. That is, you can organize your iterations under releases as illustrated in Figure 1-8. In this scenario, you are releasing goods at the end of each release, but not at each iteration. In other words, you are making sure that the end user gets a real business value at the end of each release cycle/iteration.

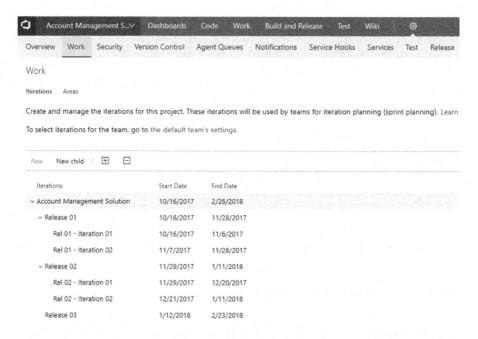

**Figure 1-8.** *Iterations grouped into releases*

You might want to have a different release cadence for your dev/ feature development team and for the support activities. For example, let's say you deliver hotfixes weekly/daily/on demand, whereas you deliver new features to the system monthly/quarterly. What are your options for handling such a situation with VSTS/TFS? In each team, you can decide which iterations are visible or which the team should work with. Here are the choices:

- *Backlog Iteration:* This allows you to set which work items appear in your backlog and boards for the team.

- *Default Iteration:* This defines which iteration the work items get assigned to if they are created from the team context.

You can select a set of iterations to appear in the backlog and the board view for iterations. Play around with the different settings to figure out the ideal setup for your team and for your team project. For example, if you have set up a release cadence comprising two iterations per one release, as shown in Figure 1-8, it is recommended that you select the iterations for your team as shown in Figure 1-9 to obtain the Work tab view shown in Figure 1-10.

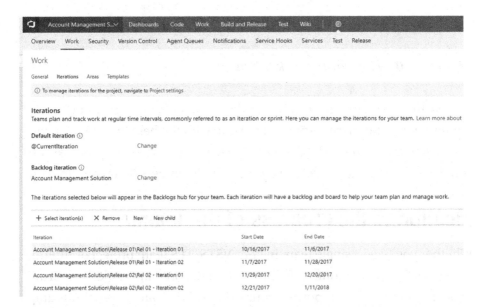

***Figure 1-9.*** *Iterations selection for the team*

Figure 1-10 shows the Backlogs view. If you inspect it carefully, note that you can see iterations belonging to two releases. Adopting naming conventions similar to those shown in this sample may help you recognize which iteration you are referring to and to which release cycle the iteration belongs.

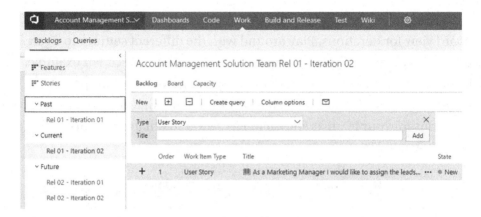

***Figure 1-10.***   *The team's Work tab view*

Assuming you use this recommended approach, make sure you remember to alter these setting to come up with the best solutions for your needs. Remember not to let the tool dictate the terms of your process; you should decide how to model the tool to suit the process that works for you.

## Monitoring the Progress of the Teams

Whether you have a single team in your VSTS/TFS team project or multiple teams, make sure to monitor the progress of the ongoing work. As a scrum master, if you are not supporting your team, so the team understands and rectifies any blockings, then your team will fail to keep the momentum going. Of course, the team may reveal these issues toward the latter part of an iteration, but you should have an easy way to identify these issues sooner rather than later. If your team does not identify these delays as early as possible and work to rectify them, you and the team will fail to deliver the project on time.

So how can you handle this? This is when you can use the reporting and work tracking capabilities of VSTS/TFS—such as queries, charts, Kanban boards, and dashboards—to track the ongoing work on a daily basis and on demand. We dive deep into this rich set of capabilities throughout the chapters in this book.

# Large Teams

In the previous section of this chapter, we discussed how to handle ideally sized Agile teams. But in some scenarios, you must manage a much larger team, maybe due to the complexity and the tight deadlines of the project/product. Some projects/products are very complex and have many modules. Others must be delivered in a short period of time with critical deadlines that must be met along the way. To meet these requirements of project/product development, you have no other option than to use a large team, which goes beyond the recommendations of the Agile practice. As the team gets bigger, naturally it leads to various complications in terms of teamwork, collaboration, communication, and other issues.

When the team gets larger and the amount of work to be delivered is huge and critical, the best way to handle the situation is to divide the work up among team members. Make sure you focus on business modules rather than technical reasons when you divide teams in this manner. Simply dividing your team into the Java-Dev team, the C# Dev team, or UI Development and Backend Development using technical reason as criteria of division does not help; we discuss this in more depth later in this chapter.

It is also vital that you make sure to monitor the work in progress for all teams at all times. If you do not, it is very likely that you will miss the deadlines or that you will run into last-minute impediments or risks within the software development process. Miscommunication among stakeholders from different subteams is another thing to keep an eye on. It is dangerous not to have a clear vision of where the project is heading. Also, when the teams start to release each of the components of the system and do the integrations between them, if you did not lay the proper plans well in advance, things get worse. In the following sections, we discuss how to divide a large team and manage it effectively and efficiently while still leveraging the features of VSTS/TFS as an application lifecycle management (ALM) tool.

# Getting Started with Large Teams

As we already discussed for small teams, you start by creating the team project. This step is pretty much the same, regardless of your team size. With the help of your technical team, you can decide on which source control and the VSTS/TFS team project template (Agile, Scrum, or CMMI) to use.

In order to avoid managerial complexities, you must make required decisions about how to execute the project/product development at very early stages of the process. For instance, let's assume the project is very complex and has several modules, such as Membership Management, Events Management, Finance Management, Case Management, and so on. In such scenarios, what is the ideal way to proceed? You should modularize the development process so that all application modules are developed in parallel by multiple teams. Having said that, the challenge is to decide on how to divide your team to deliver modules in parallel. There are various ways of doing this, and you should consider the best solution as the example we are discussing below, that gives the business value quickly to your product/project end users.

Technically inspired team members might want to divide the team based on the technical aspects. For instance, they might want to divvy up the work into categories like the following: front-end development, business process and plugin development, database development, and so on. The danger of this approach is that the whole team might eventually lose the focus of the project's business purpose and continue to focus only on its technical aspects. At all times, the aim of the team should be to deliver value to the end users. With divisions like this, you and the team are not releasing the value to the end users. Instead, your team is focused on merely completing the work assigned to them. As a result, the integration becomes tedious and causes unnecessary delays.

Therefore, the most appropriate way of dividing a team is based on the business functions of the project. For instance, you can create different teams to develop membership management, finance management, case management, events management, and so on. Each team has its own set of developers and testers and its own scrum master. Remember earlier that we created two different teams to handle development work and support work. Similarly, you can create the relevant teams under the main team project and assign the team members to each team you created. You may want to have both a development and a support subteam for each team. However, nested teams are not a possibility in VSTS or TFS, which means you *cannot* have a team structure like the one shown in Figure 1-11.

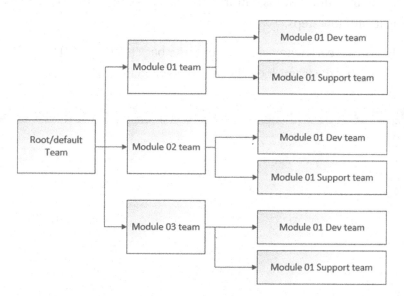

***Figure 1-11.*** *A nested team structure. This is not possible with VSTS/TFS*

In fact, it is not necessary to have such a complex team structure. Obviously, for a large team and a complex project, you might be able to have one or two separate support teams that are working on all modules support activity. So, you could set up a team for each module and then set up a support team or two under the root team.

Having said that, what should you do if you really want to have both a dev team and a support team for each of the modules because you are handling each individual module in a totally decoupled manner technically and each has independent release cadences of its own? A workaround for this is to create all required teams with areas assigned to them and then move the required module to dev team areas under the relevant module areas as children. Does this sound confusing? Let's simplify it with few steps.

1.  Create each team with an area (refer back to Figure 1-3) so that the teams look like those shown in Figure 1-12.

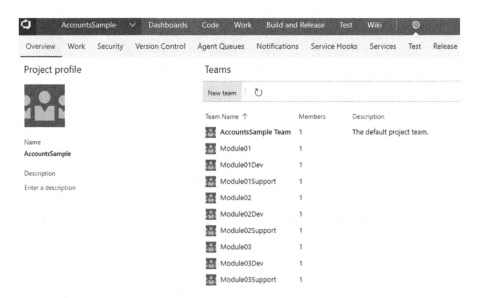

***Figure 1-12.*** *Module teams and a dev and support team for each module*

Now the areas of the team project would look like
Figure 1-13.

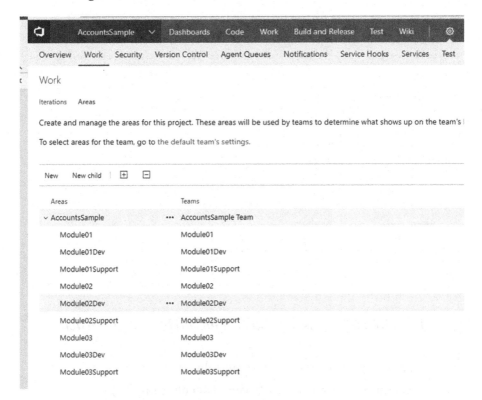

***Figure 1-13.*** *Areas created as a flat list*

2. Now drag and drop each of the module Dev and
   Support team areas to make it a child area of the
   relevant module area to achieve the nested effect
   that was not possible with teams as a default, as
   shown in Figure 1-11. This means that you will have
   an area hierarchy (as shown in Figure 1-14), instead
   of team hierarchy, to achieve the team backlog
   hierarchal structure.

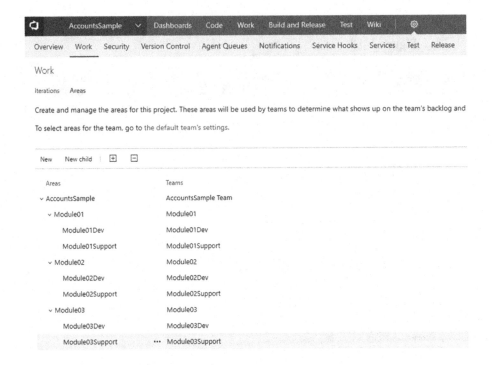

**Figure 1-14.** *Nested areas to achieve a hierarchical team structure*

For example, if you take the Module02Dev team, its default area path is `TeamProject(AccountSample)` `\Module02\Module02Dev`, as shown in Figure 1-15.

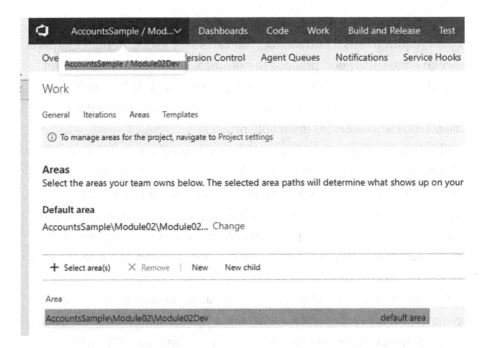

**Figure 1-15.** *Default area path of the Module02Dev team*

You can include subareas for the modules
in the team default area as discussed earlier.
So the backlog items of Module01Dev and
Module01Support team are visible in Module01.

The example shown in Figure 1-15 gives you an idea of the flexibility
of the tool, and you should configure it to accommodate your needs.
Even though many things seem impossible at first glance, after putting in
a little bit of thought and trying to change the configuration of areas and
iterations, you can achieve almost everything you need to help your team
work with a process that is best suited to them. Keep in mind that the tool
should not dictate terms to you or your team; you can change it to behave
the way you want it to since it is flexible.

You can share resources and easily add them to multiple teams based on your requirements. For instance, you can share user experience experts between teams. It is good practice to nominate someone to lead each of these teams and take ownership of the scrum master role in each team so that he or she can track the progress and communicate with the scrum master (you) who oversees the whole project.

This becomes very complicated if the team is split over different geolocations. You can follow up with the same principle to divide the teams, but remember that the team is working from different locations. Do not divide the team based on the location and assign a module; instead, always keep a mixture of people from different locations in one team that is responsible for a module. Again, you can use the Teams feature of VSTS/ TFS along with areas and iterations to manage such teams.

As explained earlier, when you create teams, behind the scenes a separate work area is created for each team you created. That is the default behavior. However, you can deselect the "Create an area path with the name of the team" checkbox that is shown in Figure 1-3 to create a team without a default area. Then you can go to the team setting and set the default area of the team to any existing area, or you can create a new area and set it to the team default area. The important thing to remember is a team must have a default area to make the backlog, boards, and so on work. You should experiment and set up the VSTS/TFS team project to your liking using the flexibility it has.

## Organizing the Backlog of Larger Teams

Because the backlog for a larger project will be so large, a flat structure of requirements is not going to work simply because multiple business functions and multiple teams will be working on those functions simultaneously. Such a scenario is when you get to use the VSTS/TFS work items (epics/features/user stories) to their full potential. For instance, you can create a hierarchy of work items as illustrated in Figure 1-16. We discuss backlog management more in Chapter 2.

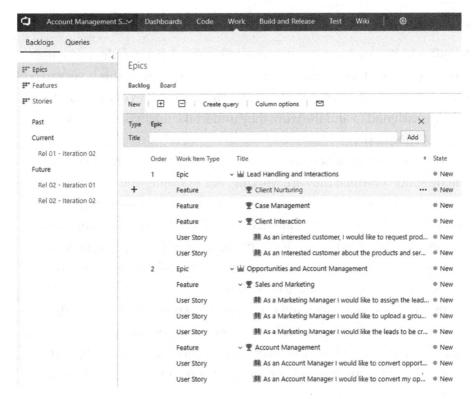

***Figure 1-16.*** *Organized backlog*

In the beginning of this section, we discussed how to divide the teams. Ideally, a larger team should be divided into multiple teams that focus on the business functionality. As explained previously, this is the appropriate method for delivering business value to the end user in large projects. As we know so far, when creating teams, behind the scene VSTS/TFS also creates the areas by default, which enables you to assign the work items to the relevant team by simply changing the area path. Now that you have set up the teams, the work items management is the next step therefore you should gain an understanding, to begin the project/product development, which we will discuss in detail in Chapter 2.

# Defining the Delivery Cadence for Multiple Teams

As with ideally sized teams, you must define the delivery cadence for the project/product development for large teams. Remember this is very tricky since different teams are going to be working on features of each module they are assigned to and the work they undertake might have different levels of complexity.

Some teams might demand a longer delivery cadence based on the functionality on which they are working. For example, one team might like to have a three-week delivery cadence and another team might like to have a four-week delivery cadence. Even though VSTS/TFS supports different lengths of iterations, if you do not properly set up iterations and manage the work, your project deleivery targets and quality of deleivery may well end up in chaos. So, to make your work simpler, set up a delivery cadence of the same length and every team will be aligned with it. This is very handy when it comes to integration because you will be releasing fully baked goods to the clients. However, this decision again depends on the technical architecture and platforms your team chooses to deliver to the project.

It is important to plan well and define what the delivery cadence is for each of your teams before you start the project. For this, you need to get the support of your technical teams and consider all aspects; for example, if you have a very loosely coupled module design that has the ability to support previous versions of other modules with newer versions of a different module, you can consider having different delivery cadences for each module. Or, you might want to work in different iteration cycles in each module but maintain the same delivery cadence for all modules. For this, you can share one level of iterations with all modules to denote releases and then have different child iterations for each module team. These are just a few ideas, but to make your iteration setup to really work, you need to figure out how you want it, and then manipulate VSTS/TFS to behave the way you want the iterations to behave.

## Monitoring the Progress of Multiple Teams

When you start executing the project/product development work, it is extremely important to know the current status of your teams. When you are executing large projects, it is vital to identify any setbacks or delays as early as possible so you can take corrective actions to mitigate the issues. As explained earlier, VSTS/TFS comes with a set of reporting tools such as queries, charts, Kanban boards, and dashboards; these enables you to stay in touch with your teams. We cover these topics in detail later in this book.

# Summary

This chapter was dedicated to how you should handle teams. We explored how you can use VSTS/TFS to set up the team project, teams, areas, and iterations. We also detailed how you can use this tool to manage ideally sized Agile teams and large-scale Agile teams. You should now have a good understanding of how to organize the team structure, and with that, we can move on to Chapter 2 in which we talk more about backlog management and how to share work with different teams.

# CHAPTER 2

# Working with a Backlog

The *backlog* is the list of items or tasks that you must complete to successfully deliver your software project/product. We briefly identified the capability VSTS/TFS offers to manage your backlog in Chapter 1. This list of work might be comprised of new features to be implemented (new requirements), alterations to existing features per feedback from stakeholders (changes to requirements), or issues (bugs) reported in already delivered components of the software that need to be fixed. The backlog has to be analyzed for business-value creation and the difficulty/risk involved in the implementation, and based on those facts, the list should be prioritized so you deliver the most valuable items first to the client. In Agile practice, you are familiar with using the backlog grooming activity to clarify and deepen the knowledge of the requirements specified in a backlog. This helps your team to identify the risks involved and the effort required in implementing the requirement.

In this chapter, we explore the essentials of managing an effective backlog to support your team to deliver the expected outcome of the software product/project. We discuss the capabilities of VSTS/TFS that enable you to leverage these to the benefit of your team.

© Chaminda Chandrasekara, Sanjaya Yapa 2018
C. Chandrasekara and S. Yapa, *Effective Team Management with VSTS and TFS*,
https://doi.org/10.1007/978-1-4842-3558-4_2

# Defining Work

*Work* is what your team has to do to deliver a software project to your client. This can be an individual development task, a business functionality requirement that needs to be implemented, a testing activity, a test case that is specified to identify how the requirement should be tested, a defect reported, and so on. These different types of work that you need to perform can be categorized into the following three main categories: The following subsections explain them briefly.

- Work that deliver value to clients

- Work that supports the work that delivers value to clients

- Work that will eventually deliver value to clients but that presently needs ground work to enable it to be implemented in the future (aka Spike items)

The following subsections explain them briefly.

# Work That Delivers Value to Clients

This type of work is the most important that you need to perform, and you should understand clearly what you need to do for each task. In general, this type of work is called *requirements of the client.* In addition to these requirements, this type of work can also include issues/defects reported in software where fixes of them also deliver a value to the client. In the Agile world, this work is called *user stories* and any issues/defects are referred to as *bugs;* in the Scrum process, you call this work *product backlog items (PBIs),* but each issue is still a bug. For the CMMI-based practices, the terminology used is slightly different; you have *requirements* as the main types of work and, again, bugs as the term used for issues or defects. In VSTS/TFS, the project templates are available with work items using the same terminology to map with Agile, Scrum, or CMMI processes. You do have flexibility to introduce your own types of work items, however; we discuss this further in Chapter 6.

## Support Work

This type of work helps you complete the work that delivers value to your client. In order to deliver requirements and defect fixes, your team needs to perform development tasks, test the requirements and defects, and so on, but this type of work also includes other supportive tasks like getting a server environment ready or providing a new laptop to your team member. This types of supportive work that your team must do needs to be handled separately from your backlog. We discussing how to handle this in future chapters.

---

**Important tip**   Of the two categories of work we just discussed, only work that delivers value to your client should be in your backlog. If you put other supportive work in your backlog, it will jeopardize the whole purpose of having a backlog. This is a common mistake made by many scrum masters and teams that you should avoid.

---

## Spike Items

You may come across some work that will eventually be valuable to your client, but that is not right now. For example, you might want to do some research on a new technological improvement that is not delivering any value to your client in its current iteration. However, you believe this research may help improve some components of your product/project in future iterations, or that it may introduce a new attractive feature to the software project that will be valuable to the client. Unlike supportive work, you should add such items to the backlog; mark/tag them as "Spike" items by using work item tags. *Work item tags* in VSTS/TFS help you filter work items in queries or in backlog, and such tags are one or two keyword phrases you use to mark/categorize work items. You can reuse a tag you define for one work item in other work items. (You can learn more about how to work with work item tags at `https://docs.microsoft.com/en-us/ vsts/work/track/add-tags-to-work-items`).

# Backlog

Although you may have your own backlog that delivers value to improve the quality of your life, in this book, we only focus on software delivery. So, in this text, the backlog we refer to involves the work that delivers value to your client business processes by providing the functionality of a software development project/product. This backlog should comprise requirements and defects to be fixed. Requirements might be vague at a software project's initial stages. For instance, you might start with just a list of user stories in a generic format, that is, *"As a person(s)*, I want *something* to happen for *some reason."* Later, you have to get clarification from your client and understand more details about the requirements. This activity is called *backlog grooming;* your team and the client should collaborate to make it a success.

## Levels of Backlog

You might want to group requirements in your backlog to clarify your requirements list. Grouping them into different levels will help you align your requirements with your product/project roadmaps. For example, let's consider a retail banking solution. This could have several modules such as Savings Accounts, Lending, Fixed Deposits, Standing Orders, and so on. The Lending module can be broken down into even smaller divisons, say Loans and Leasing. Any one of these modules might need several features implemented. For example, the Savings Accounts module may require an Account Opening feature, a Cash Withdrawal/Deposit feature, an Account Closing feature, and so on. Each of these features may also have multiple functionalities, for instance, the Account Opening feature might comprise Register Customer, Open Account, and First Cash Deposit.

How can you accommodate this requirement in VSTS/TFS? By default, VSTS/TFS has three levels—Epics, Features, and Stories/Backlog Items/ Requirements—for the backlog, and two of these three levels are already enabled (Epics is the only one that isn't). You can easily enable and disable the levels for the backlog by selecting/deselecting the checkboxes for each, as shown in Figure 2-1. If you want more levels or you want to alter the existing backlog levels, you can perform further customizations, which we discuss in Chapter 6.

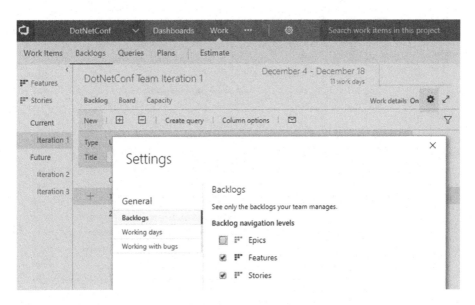

***Figure 2-1.*** *Selecting backlog levels*

Once you have the required levels enabled for your team, you can start setting up your backlog in the VSTS/TFS team project Work tab. You can add Epics and Features to group your backlog items. Then you can add Stories/Backlog Items/Requirements to your backlog.

You can group your user stories/backlog items/requirements as children of the feature work item(s) and a feature can be a child item of an epic. Figure 2-2 shows one backlog organized this way. You can also select multiple backlog items/stories and drag and drop them to reorganize by reordering or reparenting them with different features.

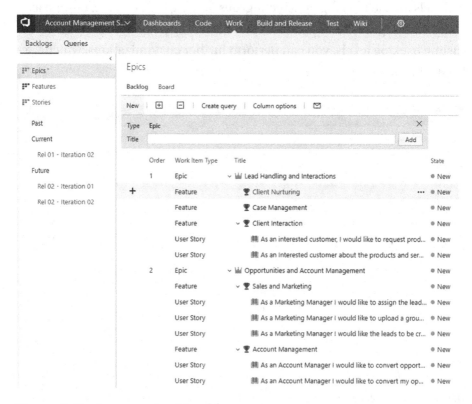

***Figure 2-2.***  *An organized backlog*

---

**Important tip**   You have the option of having a parent-child relationship among user stories (backlog items/requirements), but this kind of hierarchical backlog with one backlog level is not good practice. This is especially true in the User Story/Requirement/Backlog Item level; in this level, you must not have hierarchies, even though this is technically possible in VSTS/TFS. A flat list of user stories helps keep things simple, and it also prevents you from creating stories that violate INVEST (Independent, Negotiable, Valuable, Estimable, Small, Testable) principles (`https://xp123.com/articles/invest-in-good-stories-and-smart-tasks/`).

---

# Adding Defects/Bugs to the Backlog

Defects/bugs are detected in software once it starts getting tested at the quality assurance phase. You should add these bugs to the backlog because fixing them delivers value to your client. As a tool, VSTS/TFS allows you the flexibility to decide at which level the bugs should be handled (Figure 2-3). You have the option of keeping them in the same level of requirements, which allows you to add them as backlog items, or you can use them in the level of development or other tasks, as a child item of a requirement that needs to be done for achieving that requirement. There is also a third option—in which you do not have bugs in either backlogs or boards—but this is not a recommended approach at all.

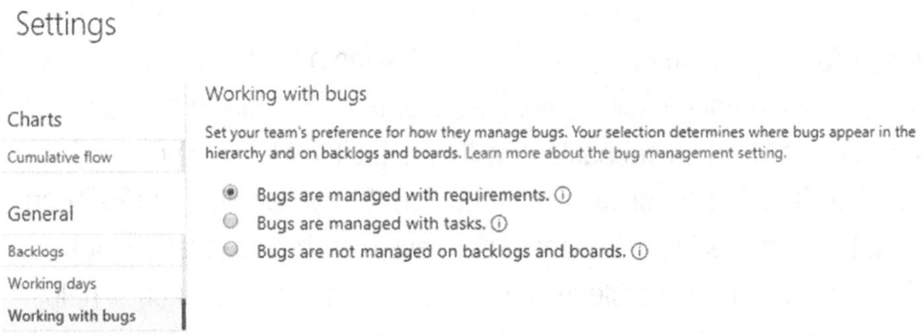

Settings

Working with bugs

Charts

Cumulative flow

Set your team's preference for how they manage bugs. Your selection determines where bugs appear in the hierarchy and on backlogs and boards. Learn more about the bug management setting.

General

   ◉ Bugs are managed with requirements. ⓘ

Backlogs

   ○ Bugs are managed with tasks. ⓘ

   ○ Bugs are not managed on backlogs and boards. ⓘ

Working days

Working with bugs

***Figure 2-3.*** *Bug management options*

If you choose to keep the bugs in the Requirements level, they are reflected in the Cumulative Flow and Velocity charts of the team. (We look at these charts in Chapter 3.) If the option of tracking the bugs with tasks is selected, you are able to reflect effort of the bugs in iteration capacity and burndown.

Out of these three options, the recommended one is to manage bugs with requirements, which allows you to execute multiple tasks to get a bug fixed. Some bugs are very complex, which means it might involve more than one task to get each fixed; it is useful to track the testing effort in another task after the bug is fixed.

# Grooming Your Backlog

Grooming the backlog plays a vital role in the successful delivery of a software project. If the team does not clearly understand the requirement, it cannot determine the technical implementation, that is, provide the customer with the expected business process flow. Because of this, it is essential that you allocate sufficient time during your project development iterations to groom your backlog.

Make sure to get your product owner (client/business analyst) to help the team groom the backlog. Remember, the priority of the backlog items belongs to your product owner. As a result, the order of the backlog is decided by the product owner. Make sure to support your team to get the items on the top of the list clarified in the backlog grooming sessions (see Figure 2-4).

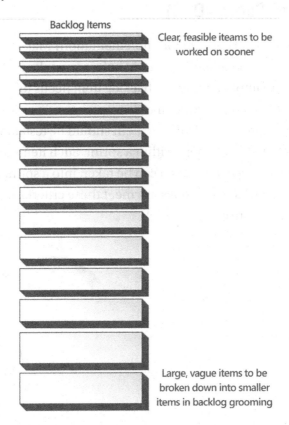

*Figure 2-4.* *The backlog*

## Definition of Done (DoD)

How do you make sure your team gets backlog items done (that is, they make sure each backlog item is developed, tested, and ready for production)? The key is the acceptance criteria for the backlog items. When you collaboratively define acceptance criteria with your product owner, your team should understand the real requirement.

This collaboration and understanding minimizes the risk and drastically improves your team's chance of delivering a requirement successfully.

## Definition of Ready (DoR)

How ready is your backlog item for implementation? Make sure your backlog items meet the following criteria before you take each into an iteration/sprint to implement it: the backlog item needs to be clear and understood by the team, it should have acceptance criteria that is defined so that everyone agrees on a DoD; the item should be testable; and it should be feasible to implement within a sprint. Such items are referred to as *DoR-met backlog items*, which can be taken into a sprint as shown in Figure 2-5. If the backlog item does not meet these criteria, it should be broken down to a more granular level.

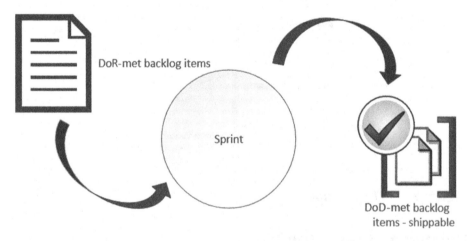

*Figure 2-5.* *DoR vs. DoD*

# Using Work Item Fields

You can use the fields in the VSTS/TFS work items to provide more clarity for your backlog items. Let's discuss a few such important fields.

- *Acceptance Criteria:* As discussed earlier, this is the most important field in any backlog item (user story/backlog item/requirement and bug work items). This field defines the criteria that must be met before the customer accepts the item as done. It is important to have clear criteria defined in this field to ensure that the entire team knows exactly what the conditions are that should be satisfied in the implementation.

- *Story Points/Effort/Size:* This field contains the relative effort estimation as a numeric value. It can be defined with any numeric unit of measurement that your team prefers to use. This is the Agile/Scrum relative size value used to identify the team velocity or in other words how much work (total effort) the team can perform. VSTS/TFS has automated velocity charts and the capability to forecast the amount of work that can be delivered in each iteration, which we discuss later. You can learn more about team velocity here: www.agilealliance.org/glossary/velocity.

- *Title:* This field briefly explains what the backlog item is. For stories/requirements, you can use the format of "As a *person(s)*, I want *something* to happen for *some reason*." For bugs, you can use the same format or just a few words to clarify what the issue is.

- *Description:* This field should address three major questions: why, what, and for whom this item should be implemented. How it should be implemented should not be included here; instead this should be described with the child tasks defined to implement the story or fix the bug. The team should be able to define test cases and tasks based on the description of the backlog item.

- *Iteration Path:* Iteration defines where the backlog item belongs. When you define a backlog, normally it should be at the root of a team project, meaning the team project name would be the iteration path. We discuss the other alternatives in Chapter 3.

- *Area Path:* This field defines which team or which specific submodule the backlog item belongs to. As we discussed in Chapter 1, depending on the setting you have established for each team, the visibility of backlog items changes when you set the iteration path. We cover how to use this field more in Chapter 3.

- *Priority:* Rating of the requirement or bug related to the business is defined in this field. Allowed values are 1, 2, and 3, which have the following specific meanings; the default value is 2.

    1. Cannot ship without implementing this story or fixing the bug.

    2. Cannot ship without the item, but this value is not needed to attend to this item immediately.

    3. This value is optional to implement based on the risk and resource availability.

The preceding fields are a common set that you can use, but there are specific fields in each work item type—for example, repro steps field in bugs helps to capture the steps on how to reproduce a given bug.

## Using Test Cases and Tasks

The test case should describe what the expected implementation of the backlog item is and how it will be tested. To make the implementation successful, it is vital that you write test cases as much as possible before you implement the backlog item. However, it is okay to add more test cases even after implementation as the actual testing occurs, because new scenarios that were not predicted before may be visible at this point. In VSTS/TFS, test cases are added to a user story/backlog item/requirement or even to a bug with a special relationship link called "tested by." From the test case perspective, the relationship is called "tests." For example, a story is tested by a test case and a test case tests the user story.

In VSTS/TSF, Task (the Task work item) should be a child relationship with the backlog items or bugs set to behave as backlog items. This is possible only if "Bugs are managed with requirements" is selected under the Product Backlog settings.

A task should describe the full or partial implementation of the backlog item and how it should be implemented. If it is a small implementation, one task may be sufficient for describing how the backlog item should be implemented. If a single task cannot do the full implementation, multiple tasks can be used to describe the details of implementation by dividing work among the tasks. In a practical scenario, the team focuses on completing a task within six hours, and during the estimation, if it is evident that it is going to take more than six hours, then the team must divide the task into multiple tasks. There can be tasks other than the implementation/development of a backlog item such as test case writing tasks, testing tasks, test automation development tasks, and so on. You can use Activity field of the task to identify the type of task to which the task can be linked with team capacity as described later in this chapter.

# Prioritizing the Backlog

Your team should be involved in grooming the backlog. This means that they may be introducing new stories and breaking down product-owner-defined large stories, into smaller, testable, and feasible stories. However, which story/backlog item should be considered for development first is totally owned by the product owner or your client. Hence, prioritizing the backlog is neither your responsibility nor something you or your team should do.

So how can you make sure the items are implementation ready according to the priority of your client? Make sure your team always focuses on the top of the backlog when it is performing the grooming activity. If you must break a larger story into smaller stories, communicate to the product owner that you have made a few stories out of one to make the project more feasible. The product owner may then reprioritize the stories/backlog items. In VSTS/TFS, to prioritize the backlog items, the product owner can drag and drop items in the preferred order so that the topmost items are the highest priority items and the priority order is identified as top to bottom.

# Estimating Your Backlog Work

Estimating work plays an important part in project delivery. In Agile development, empowering your team and identifying their *velocity* (how much they can deliver in an iteration) is vital. To prevent yourself (as the scrum master) from micromanaging the team, you should focus on a few things, especially when you are estimating tasks.

Keeping this in mind, let's look at what the options are for estimating work. You are already familiar with estimating using relative sizes for backlog items in general Agile/Scrum practices. In the previous section, we discussed the Story Points/Effort/Size work item field as being the field you use to capture the relative size of a backlog item. Relative estimation is described here: www.agilealliance.org/glossary/relative-estimation/. There is one limitation in VSTS/TFS when it comes to relative estimation; you must always use a numeric scale to estimate relatively. It can be any numeric scale of your choice. There are few free extensions in Visual Studio Marketplace (`https://marketplace.visualstudio.com/search?term=es timate&target=VSTS&category=All%20categories&sortBy=Relevance`) to get relative estimation built into your VSTS/TFS backlog. Out of these, the extension developed by Microsoft DevLabs, is effective and integrates well with the backlog items so you and your team can play planning poker (relative estimation game to size the stories with team input) on the backlog (`https://marketplace.visualstudio.com/items?itemName=ms-devlabs. estimate`). You can select a work item and vote for it as a team and play planning pocker online; once all members vote, you can reveal the votes, discuss, and revote if you need to (Figure 2-6). Extensions enable you to record the average estimation (you can edit this value) in the story point of the backlog item.

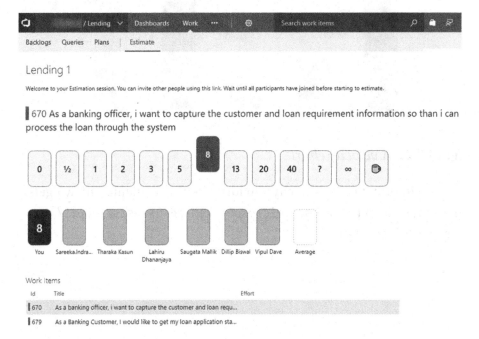

***Figure 2-6.*** *Estimating the backlog items*

For now, let's skip the topic of estimating tasks since it is more relevant to work in the iteration. We discuss tasks and task estimation in detail later in this chapter.

The benefit of estimating your backlog items with a relative size is that VSTS/TFS provides you with a velocity chart for each iteration. A green color indicates the cumulative size of all stories/backlog items that have been completed. Blue shows the total size of all items that have had work started on them but that have not yet been completed within the iteration. In Figure 2-7 the last iteration is still in progress and a considerable amount of work still needs to be completed.

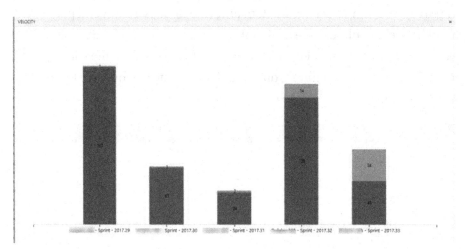

***Figure 2-7.*** *A velocity chart*

More information on velocity and further enhancements with widgets can be found at https://docs.microsoft.com/en-us/vsts/report/dashboards/team-velocity.

# Getting Stakeholder Feedback

Feedback is vital in order to understand the stakeholder expectations. A stakeholder may want to give feedback on a user story or on the application itself. This can take the form of just feedback or it might be a bug reported by the client. Your team may also want to request feedback from your client on the application or on a user story/backlog item.

VSTS/TFS provides rich functionality for enabling all such scenarios. For instance, your stakeholders can add an extension to their browser from https://marketplace.visualstudio.com/items?itemName=ms. vss-exploratorytesting-web. This extension allows your stakeholders to use a browser to provide feedback on the application or report bugs. The extension should be connected with VSTS/TFS and if a bug is reported using this extension, it appears on your team's backlog. In addition to reporting bugs, stakeholders can create test cases or tasks using the Test and Feedback extension, as shown in Figure 2-8. When feedback is provided without a feedback request, it is identified as *voluntary feedback.*

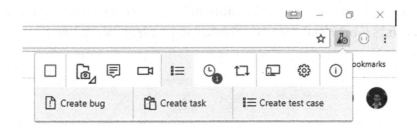

***Figure 2-8.*** *The Test and Feedback browser extension*

In the VSTS/TFS web portal, there is an option to request feedback, and when such a request is made, stakeholders can provide feedback for the request (https://docs.microsoft.com/en-us/vsts/manual-test/ stakeholder/provide-stakeholder-feedback#provide).

# Defining a Process

How your team wants to work with the backlog is another important aspect that you should help them identify. *Kanban boards* help you define this process for your backlog items. The process can be as simple as

- New ➤ Active ➤ Resolved➤ Closed workflow

or something like this:

- New ➤ Ready ➤ Solutioning ➤ DevReady ➤ Active ➤ Testing ➤ DeployedStaging ➤ ProductionDeployed

VSTS/TFS provides you with a Kanban board for backlog in which you can define your own columns. You must have a start column and an end column that are set to the New and Closed states, and then you can alter the middle set of columns, allow them to be used, and set the work item state of your preference (Figure 2-9). For each column, you have to define the state of each backlog item type to be used. You have the ability to introduce your custom states to work items, which we discuss in Chapter 6. You can learn how to add/edit columns at `https://docs.microsoft.com/en-us/vsts/work/kanban/add-columns#add-or-rename-columns`.

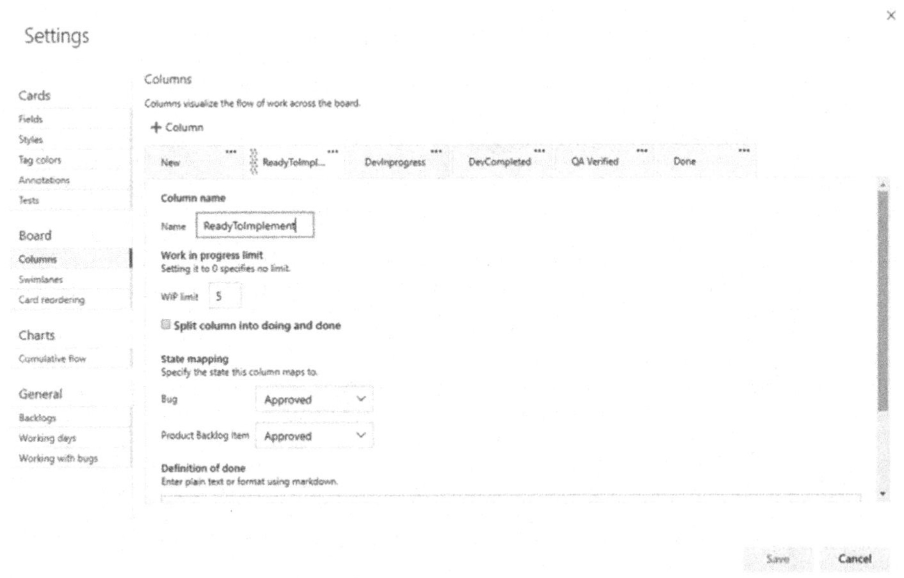

**Figure 2-9.**  *Kanban board customization*

Another important aspect of effective team management is limiting your work in progress no matter what the process is that you are following. If your team has four developers and you have each working on a different backlog item, this is not going to help in achieving iteration goal. Instead, help your team pick the topmost items from the backlog, and make sure they finish them before they move down the backlog order. The idea is that this helps a team move the backlog items from left to right in the Kanban board as soon as possible. Having too many items and too much work in progress may end up in disaster because your team will have nothing totally completed by the end of an iteration. Having 99 percent completed is not valuable as an iteration goal. We discuss this more in Chapter 3. VSTS/TFS Kanban boards help you set a work-in-progress (WIP) limit for each column and indicate in red if you have gone past the number, as shown in Figure 2-10.

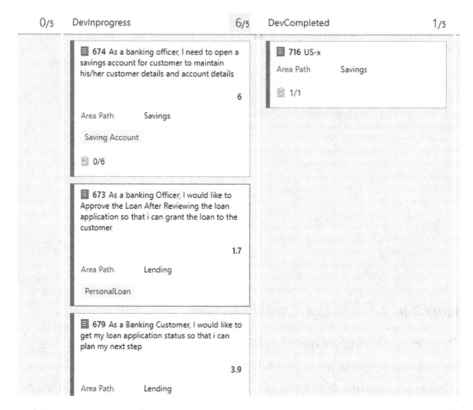

***Figure 2-10.*** *WIP limit exceeded*

You can define the DoD for each of the columns in order to define what the criteria is to move to the next column. Also, you are able to split a column on the Kanban board into work-in-progress and work-completed sections. Let's say you want to move fast with a few backlog items and you give them high priority for some reason; in such a case, you can use swimlanes feature on the Kanban board to introduce an expedited swimlane (horizontal row accross "in progress" state columns of the Kanaban board). A backlog item shown on Kanban board is called a *card*. You have the option of defining which fields you want the card to show on your board (Figure 2-11). For more information on the Kanban board of VSTS/TFS refer to "Filter Your Kanban Board" under "How-to Guides" at https://docs.microsoft.com/en-us/vsts/work/kanban/filter-kanban-board.

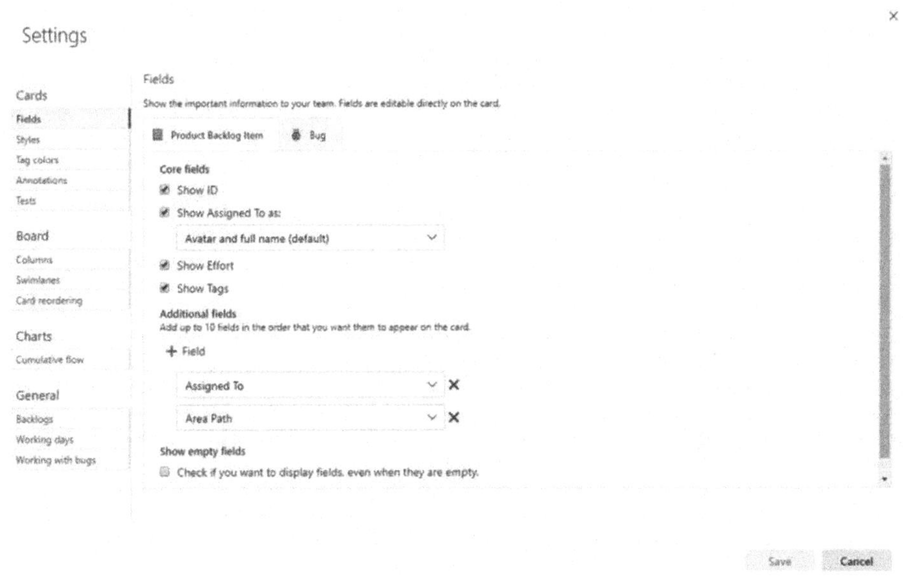

Settings                                                                    ×

Cards

   Fields

   Styles

   Tag colors

   Annotations

   Tests

Board

   Columns

   Swimlanes

   Card reordering

Charts

   Cumulative flow

General

   Backlogs

   Working days

   Working with bugs

Fields

Show the important information to your team. Fields are editable directly on the card.

▦ Product Backlog Item     🐞 Bug

Core fields

☑ Show ID

☑ Show Assigned To as:

   Avatar and full name (default)                    ∨

☑ Show Effort

☑ Show Tags

Additional fields
Add up to 10 fields in the order that you want them to appear on the card.

+ Field

   Assigned To                                      ∨  ✕

   Area Path                                        ∨  ✕

Show empty fields

☐ Check if you want to display fields, even when they are empty.

Save     Cancel

***Figure 2-11.** Card fields*

A Kanban board can be used to provide more information visually. For instance, you can set different card and text colors to get your team's attention on the required items. For example, let's say a backlog item is staying on the backlog longer than a week as a development in progress and it is an alarm to your team, which is indicating possible failure of achieving the iteration goal. The VSTS/TFS card style rules will help you indicate such cases visually in the Kanban board as shown in Figure 2-12.

*Figure 2-12.*  *Card style rules*

So far, we have only discussed the backlog and Kanban board and have not yet discussed the task board details. For a focus on the task board, refer to Chapter 3, where we discuss the execution of an iteration.

# Planning with a Small Team

We discussed ideal-sized Agile teams in Chapter 1, and we identified the advantage of using the team concept in VSTS/TFS, that is, to have a Developmental (Dev) team and a Support team. With this approach, you can have a different workflow in your Kanban board at the Root/Default or Team Project level and two different workflows for the Dev team and Support team on their Kanban boards. This is because you can set up Kanban columns based on the team.

The advantage of this is from the Team Project perspective; you might want to monitor both the Dev team and Support team work. For instance, team project root team Kanban board would be a combination of Kanban columns of both the teams or a subset of columns for the teams. The Dev team and the Support team might require different approaches, and you can decide columns based on each team's requirement.

You might want to work in the same release cadence or different release cadences for the two teams. You can set up the iterations for each team by selecting the required iterations to appear in the backlog, as we discussed in Chapter 1. The Area Path of each team helps you distinguish each team's backlog and isolate one from the other.

Let's take one team's perspective and analyze what it needs to do to be effective. It already has a backlog in place and has test cases defined for top level backlog items. The team has its backlog items in the ready state (DoR) for development with clear acceptance criteria (DoD). The backlog is prioritized by the product owner and the team has performed relative estimations on the backlog items. From this point, teams first task is to select backlog items from the top of backlog for the first iteration. The team should do this in an Agile/ Scrum sprint planning session if it is following one of those processes.

## Task Estimations

It is at this point in the process that you and your team might make a lot of mistakes. Since VSTS/TFS supports hour-based estimates, you may want to use hours to recrd effort for a task. Then you might start monitoring team members to see whether they put the right number of hours toward each task as they complete the task. Eventually the individual goal focus will develop over the team goal. But a sprint burndown chart (we discuss the burndown chart more in Chapter 3, but you can also find out more at https://docs.microsoft.com/en-us/vsts/work/scrum/sprint-burndown) would be useful, wouldn't it? How about a story point/size/effort (Backlog item relative effort value) burndown (Figure 2-13)? Sounds great, but how can you do it? Let's look at the possibilities here.

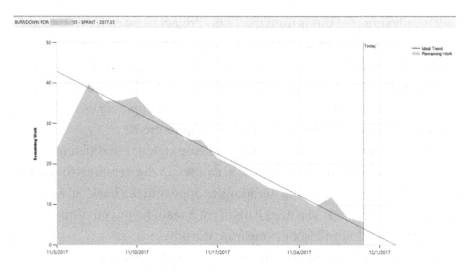

**Figure 2-13.** *Story point burndown*

To estimate how long a task will take, you can use the simplest mechanism—just divide the backlog item size/effort/story points by a number of tasks, and assign each of the tasks an Original Estimate value and Remaining Work value before the work starts, as the resultant value. You may argue that the effort value should not be equal to each of the tasks as task complexity might differ from task to task and would take a different amount of effort to achieve. But the thinking here is that the backlog item is done when all tasks are 100 percent complete. So, you do not really need to do complex estimations and waste your team's time. Another advantage to this estimation of tasks is that it can be fully automated. You can create a simple PowerShell script to call the REST API of VSTS/TFS and autocalculate the task estimations; you can then assign the autocalculated task effort value via the script to each task's Original Estimate and Remaining Work fields. Then you can run this script with a scheduled build each day 15–30 minutes before midnight (or you can let it run every 2 hours or so to get more accuracy) to recalculate task estimation based on the number of tasks and the available estimate value in backlog item for each backlog item in the current iteration. You can enhance this script to assure that the Remaining Work value of the tasks that are in a Closed state is set to zero.

This is a practically tested formula for a few teams and it works really well for two main reasons: one, it is simple to understand and implement; and two, the team does not have to waste time on estimating tasks after they estimate the backlog items relatively. If the task effort value calulation and assignment are automated with scripts, the formula works even better, since team members just have to close the respective tasks once they are done to get a burndown working. Even the addition of a new task to the backlog item in the middle of the sprint does not require a manual calculation because the script takes care of it and assigns effort with a recalculation. We further discuss practical usage and the advantages of this approach in Chapter 3.

One other important aspect of being effective in managing teams while using VSTS/TFS as a tool, is the size of the tasks you define to implement the backlog items. Generally, a task should fit within a day, meaning the task should be accomplished within a day or less. A task that expands to more than a day mostly likely is not defined well enough and is vague. In general, if a task is defined with a clear DoD and technical implementation details for a backlog item that is groomed and sized properly, it should fit within a day. You have to make sure your team understands this fact and breaks the tasks into achievable, granular levels. There can be some exceptions to this, but the majority of the tasks should be achievable within a day.

## Capacity Planning

You should know how much effort capacity you have within your team. This information gives you insight into how much work you can take on with the team for a given iteration. Especially if you share resources among Dev and Support teams in your project, this knowledge helps prevent overallocation. VSTS/TFS provides rich feature capability to allow for capacity planning in your iterations (`https://docs.microsoft.com/en-us/vsts/work/scale/capacity-planning`). Again, for this, use the same unit you have used for the backlog item in your relative estimation. Define a rough value for each team member of how many story points/ size/effort he/she can do per day. Remember to avoid using hours as your units—we discussed the disadvantages of the hour-based task estimation in the previous section. You have the capability to define team off days and team member holidays, and you can even define how much capacity you have based on activity type (development, testing, and so on). This activity type is linked with the Activity field of your Task work items and this gives valuable information to the team about the capacity they have for a given iteration (the Iteration backlog view) with respect to the activities and task requirements shown in Figure 2-14.

***Figure 2-14.*** *Capacity*

# Planning with a Large Team

All that we discussed in ideal-sized teams applies to large teams as well, with the exception that you are applying all of this information to small teams within a large team. Make sure to use the Area Path to separate each team's backlog from the other teams' and that you share the same iterations for all teams or that you use different iterations for each team depending on your requirements. We discussed iterations for large teams in Chapter 1.

If your team is distributed in different geolocations and in different time zones, you might have a bit of an issue with burndown charts and the like depending on the default time zone setting in your TFS server or your VSTS account. The problem is that a team that is working in a different time zone from VSTS/TFS will not really start or end their work day so that it matches the start and end of the day shown in burndown or iteration. The ideal solution is to set up a preferred time zone for each team, but unfortunately no such feature is available in VSTS/TFS as of the writing of this book. If such a feature did exist, you could go against the rules we discussed in Chapter 1—you could mix different geolocation members within teams and use separate teams for each geolocation. But considering the facts, as we discussed them in Chapter 1, mixing the team with a bit of discrepancy in the start and end time of the work day is worthwhile for distributed teams.

# Visualizing Your Plan

Another valuable extension you can add to your VSTS/TFS is named Delivery Plans, which allows you to visualize the work status of your teams and team projects on an iteration-based calendar (https://marketplace.visualstudio.com/items?itemName=ms.vss-plans). You can set markers for important dates and add filter criteria to filter work items to be shown in the plan. You can learn more about delivery plans in https://docs.microsoft.com/en-us/vsts/work/scale/review-team-plans; we discuss the effective usage of these in Chapter 5.

# The Sprint Zero or the Pre-Sprint

The sprint zero/no-sprint/pre-sprint is the initial time of a project where you set up the solution structure, get the development machines ready, and so on. An essential part of the start of a project is to set up the build deployment pipelines (the continuous integration and continuous delivery [CI/CD] pipelines). You can learn all the basics you need to implement successful build and release pipelines in one of the co-author's books, *Beginning Build and Release Management with TFS 2017 and VSTS*, which is available at www.apress.com/in/book/9781484228104.

You should also get all your test and deployment environments ready before your project/product development sprints start. This enables your team to focus on implementing customer requirements rather than worrying about how to get the work deployed or tested. Many Agile starting teams have failed because they have not identified how important the level of automation is to be really agile.

# Summary

In this chapter, we explored how to set up a proper backlog and backlog tasks for your teams. We identified many features in VSTS/TFS to help you set up your required backlog and to help you track and visualize the work your team is planning to do. We also discussed common mistakes you may make due to the overwhelming capabilities of VSTS/TFS, and we especially focused on how you can avoid the micromanagement that results from misuse of features.

In the next chapter, you learn how to leverage VSTS/TFS features to empower your team while executing a project iteration.

# CHAPTER 3

# Working on the Iteration

In the previous two chapters, we discussed how to set up the project, populate the backlog, define the delivery cadence, create teams, plan for the team process, groom the backlog, prioritize the backlog items, size the requirements, and plan the iteration. We even discussed getting things in place—such as a solutions structure, build and deployment pipelines, and testing environments—in a pre-iteration time period. Doing all of this prior to the first iteration enables your team to focus more singlemindedly on implementing backlog items once you kick off project work, but while making sure to allocate sufficient time for backlog grooming. In previous chapters, we also discussed the challenges faced by both ideal-sized and large teams during this initial planning stage and how you and your team can use VSTS/TFS features effectively to overcome these challenges.

This chapter is dedicated to executing a project, starting with the first iteration, and it provides practical solutions to common challenges the team faces when using VSTS/TFS. We discuss the following in detail:

- Getting ready for the iteration and daily activity

- Tracking and resolving roadblocks and performing other supportive work

- Working with code and testing the work

© Chaminda Chandrasekara, Sanjaya Yapa 2018
C. Chandrasekara and S. Yapa, *Effective Team Management with VSTS and TFS*,
https://doi.org/10.1007/978-1-4842-3558-4_3

- Exploring progress-monitoring options

- Avoiding rather than fixing defects

- Facilitating unavoidable and mandatory fixes

- Handling disaster situations during the iteration

- Ensuring the stability of the releases

- Visualizing the iteration and positively impacting the team

# Starting the Sprint

Now everything is set for you to start your first sprint. That is, your team has decided what to deliver by the end of the new sprint by selecting a few backlog items for the sprint from the top of the backlog. As we discussed in Chapter 2, you should have tasks defined for each of the backlog items to help get them completed. Make sure you have estimated task efforts by simply dividing the relative size of backlog items (story points/effort) by the number of tasks each contains. You have probably already automated this process, as we recommended in Chapter 2.

Make absolutely sure you have determined each individual team member's capacity using the same scale that you used to relatively estimate backlog items. Again, capacity should have been assigned according to the activity type, as we discussed in Chapter 2. Make sure the available capacity to complete each activity (development, testing, etc.) for the iteration is visible to the entire team in a number of story points/sizes.

Make sure to have your solution architecture ready to start development work. Another thing that you must understand is that solution architecture is not similar to the foundation of some construction project. Because a building is planned fully ahead of time and is constructed according to this plan, it can have a fixed foundation. Software, on the other hand, always has to evolve depending on customer needs as well as technological changes. So, the architecture of a solution should also be flexible so it can evolve and improve as the software project/product gets developed. That does not mean your team should not consider platform, tools or architecture when building software. The team should plan for suitable platforms, a technological architecture, and development tools with the current knowledge it has about the system that needs to be implemented. But at the same time, the team should have the flexibility to let the solution architecture evolve and be willing to adapt to new platforms or other technologies as the software system matures and as more of the customer's requirements get identified and developed.

Your team should have a sufficient number of test cases developed for the backlog items in the iteration by now. But that is, of course, the ideal situation, and maybe your team has more work to do in the iteration. This is fine as long as the team has enough details in the backlog items and well-defined acceptance criteria, with tasks defined to describe the implementation. Based on these, the team can add more test cases to the backlog items during the iteration. However, at a minimum, having at least a few test cases that describe how to test the backlog item's main scenarios definitely helps the team progress with the implementation.

It is important to get the development environments ready, before the start of the iteration, with the required development tools, software development kits (SDKs), and any other additional tools your team needs. Your team might discover more tools and platform it needs during the iteration as the software project evolves; we discuss how to handle such situations later in this chapter.

The other most important task you need to perform before you begin the iteration is getting the testing environments ready to start testing the software components once their development is complete. Your team has to get the packaging and deployment of the software automated and deploy it to another environment for testing. Again, it is okay if not all these tasks are fully completed before the start of the project development work with the first iteration. We discuss how to handle such tasks and how to automate the packaging and deployment of software components later in this chapter.

Make sure you utilize your team members effectively to accomplish all the tasks mentioned so far. Remember that these activities are different from and are in addition to the main backlog item implementations. Your team also has to perform backlog grooming activities in your main backlog to get the items ready for future iterations. For all these reasons, the team needs a significant amount of time, and you should keep all these facts in mind when you are setting up capacity for individual members of the team. Allow the team members having more reduced capacity in the initial iterations, partially because there might be more non-backlog implementation work in the initial stages of a project/product implementations.

You may think that setting up environments, setting up build release pipelines, or activities associated with backlog grooming should also be in the backlog so you can track them and know how many resources they are consuming, but in fact, this not good practice. You need to remember that these are supportive activities that are not generating value to the customer directly. These activities should not be in the main product backlog, and although you should track them, you should do so separately from the main backlog; we discuss this further in a later section of this chapter.

# Daily Activity

Prior to beginning each iteration—regardless of whether it is the first, a middle one, or the last one in the project's life—you and your team need to do some quick planning for the day to ensure effective execution.

## Planning the Day

Most likely, you are already familiar with the daily stand-up or daily scrum, which is a 15-minute time-boxed event. Planning for a day does not need more than 15 minutes since you already have a well-groomed backlog in place and the team knows what is in their hands to deliver.

The general questions defined in such scrums are these:

- What did I do yesterday?

- What will I do today?

- Are there any roadblocks?

Always make sure the discussion of these questions is conducted from the perspective of the team's goals rather than personal goals. Take this time to focus your team and empower them; let them strive toward the team goal. If you make this quick discussion on a course of action for the day into a daily update on the status of individuals, each team member will only worry about getting individual tasks done and about the number of tasks on her shoulders. Team members will not focus, as they should, on the team goal of getting backlog items done or on helping each other get them done. Individual performance is important, but getting the team to collaboratively and supportively work together, targeting backlog items to be completed, is what makes the project a success. Having said that, it is okay to use the sprint board and change the status of tasks during the daily stand-up. Ideally the team should not wait until the stand-up to make status changes or other updates to the work items, however.

So, this meeting is not a time for each team member to state, "I have done this and that, and I will do this today," to make their individual profile impressive. After all, consider that team member who helped another member who was struggling with a task due to a technical difficulty; the helping team member has nothing of her own to declare accomplished, so she might get embarrassed. You should encourage team members to help others, but do not allow a team member to declare that he just helped another and could not get any of his own work done for days. Helping others toward an iteration goal is good, but team members cannot just do nothing on their own goals by claiming that they were helping others all the time, because this adversely affects the team goals.

VSTS/TFS provides a board (sprint board) for sprint execution, which you can use for planning the day, review the past day, and seeing whether the team is marching forward toward the iteration goal of getting the selected backlog items done. You can set up rules similar to the backlog board card style rules we discussed in Chapter 2 to visualize the work that is done and to highlight any bottlenecks with different colors (Figure 3-1). To set up rules, go to Settings page of the relevant board.

*Figure 3-1.*  *Taskboard rules*

Visualizing the task states and story progress in boards reduces the time of the stand-up meeting because no one needs to ask what each individual has done, because it is indicated on the board in colors. For example, Figure 3-2 shows tasks that have been in progress for more than two days in red.

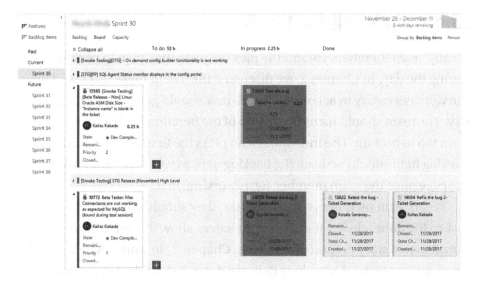

***Figure 3-2.*** *Taskboard indicating tasks not moving forward*

In addition to the task/iteration board, the team should also look at the backlog board. It offers insight to the team on how they are progressing with the backlog. They can use style rules to highlight current sprint backlog items and can even indicate items waiting in the "in progress" state for a longer time. Additionally, story point burndown, as we discussed in Chapter 2, can also provide valuable information to the team in daily planning and help identify the team's ability to get the work completed on time.

In the daily stand-up, the team should bring forward any impediments/roadblocks that are affecting team progress. These issues should be handled separately from the main backlog, however; we discuss them later in this chapter.

# Choosing Work for the Day

Ideally, team members voluntarily pick the tasks they plan to perform during the day. In Chapter 2, we discussed the size of these tasks, and how the work necessary to accomplish each task should generally fit within a day. The team should focus on the top of the iteration backlog and work from top to bottom. The individual who picks the first task of a particular backlog item should activate the backlog item as well. The task must be set to active once the team member starts working on it.

When team members complete tasks, they should change the task to the done/closed state. These practices allow the automated burndown of story points (discussed in Chapter 2) to work. Once all the development tasks of a backlog item are done, it should be moved to a resolved/committed state or any other custom state that represents that development is done and testing has been started. When a backlog item is ready to be closed, some prefer to keep it active until it reaches production. You can have a custom set of columns on the board that show exactly to which environment the backlog item is currently deployed and that it is working as expected. You are able to introduce custom states to represent the same types of stages; we discuss these in Chapter 6.

Getting the first few backlog items done and moved to the testing phase takes a couple of days in any given iteration. So, in the first few days, quality assurance (QA) members of the team might have to work on getting more test cases added to the backlog items in the iteration, getting prepared for implementing test automation, and helping the development members. How to help development members is discussed later in the chapter. Additionally, QA members can look at the main backlog and review the items to help the team groom the backlog.

What we've just described is a typical situation, because, in reality, it is really hard to find multiskilled team members. If all of your team members have the ability to code, test, and do other tasks as well, that would be ideal, because then anyone can pick any type of the tasks. This situation is rare, though.

Make sure to encourage the team to do deployments to test environments as much as possible during an iteration. This requires the team to have automated deployments in place to support the frequent deployments with stability. Remember that your team may discover bugs while testing the newly built backlog items. Your team must fix these bugs within the iteration and they should be added to the iteration backlog, just below the relevant backlog item. The relevant backlog item should not be considered ready for production until all bugs have been found in testing and are fixed. The team should not expect such bugs to be considered additional work or new backlog issues that have been added to iteration; these bugs do not remove items from the bottom of backlog as the team is not meant to create the bugs in the first place if they carefully implement the backlog items properly. There can, however, be very rare exceptions to this that we discuss later in this chapter.

Make sure the entire team, with the support of the product owner, participates in regular backlog grooming sessions. Due to current iteration goals, you should not skip this activity, as doing so is apt to create bigger problems for future iterations when team members have unclear backlog items to work on. Grooming sessions do not have to happen daily but should happen regularly to make sure sufficient backlog for future iterations is groomed before the start date of those iterations is reached. Ideally close to 10 percent of iteration time duration should be spent on backlog grooming.

# Tracking and Resolving Impediments and Other Supportive Work

As we discussed in Chapter 2 and in previous sections of this chapter, some tasks support the implementation of other backlog items, such as getting a test environment ready, implementing build release pipelines, or removing any other roadblocks the team encounters while trying to progress with their work in the backlog. Some of these tasks may get reported in the daily stand-up meetings and some may be identified well before the project starts.

As you can see, these tasks can be divided into two categories: one is the roadblocks/impediments identified during project execution, such as a developer machine does not have enough RAM, a license needs to be purchased for a software tool, and so on; the other category is things that would improve and help the team continue the project execution, such as setting up the testing or staging environment or getting a build release pipeline implemented to automate deployments. Again, purchasing machines in a cloud platform or creating virtual machines inside the on-premises servers in order to set up the testing or staging environment falls under the first category of roadblocks/impediments. After the team gets the virtual machines, setting up the testing or staging environment is work that needs to be carried out by the team. The team may have to get the automated deployments working for the environment.

As you can see, roadblocks/impediments need some external support to get resolved, whereas the other supportive work to implement the backlog can be handled mostly by the team. There is no hard-fixed rule, but generally, these two types of work are differentiated.

# Handling Supportive Work within the Team

First, let's look at how to get done the work that the team has to do. You may want to add this work to the backlog, and the problem with that is your customer/product owner is apt to be confused by work internal to the team that appears in the backlog.

However, you can consider making a separate backlog of tasks for your team project. You can keep track of this work to be executed by defining it with an isolated area path that you make invisible to your customer/product owner by deselecting it for the default/root team of the team project. This way it does not appear in the main backlog.

Let's clarify this with an example setup. First, set up an area for extra activities (see Figure 3-3).

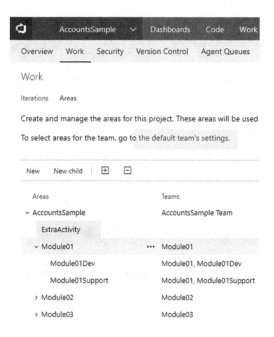

***Figure 3-3.*** *Defining an ExtraActivity area*

Then, set up the default team with areas you want to be visible other than the ExtraActivity area (Figure 3-4). This makes work items under the ExtraActivity area that are not visible to the main backlog so the product owner does not see these ExtraActivity work items. For this ExtraActivity area, you can set up a separate team if you prefer to handle this work separately from your development iterations. If you want to include them in your development team backlog, make sure the ExtraActivity area is selected for the development team. This way you can handle these activities with the team capacity but without confusing your product owner.

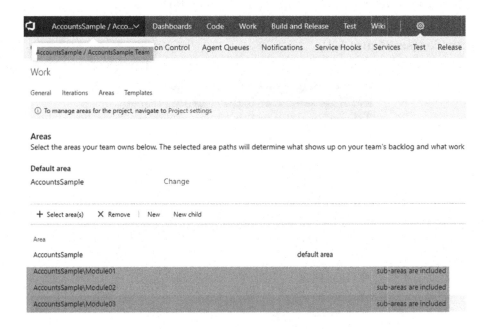

***Figure 3-4.*** *Default team without ExtraActivity area*

Additionally, you can skip the ExtraActivity work items visibility to the Delivery Plans feature, which we discussed in Chapter 2, by adding a tag to the backlog items in this area and by adding criteria to omit the tag in the plan. The tag should be used since Area Path is not currently supported in the Delivery Plan feature field criteria, as shown in Figure 3-5 (`https://docs.microsoft.com/en-us/vsts/work/scale/review-team-plans#edit-a-plan-add-field-criteria-customize-cards-and-add-markers`).

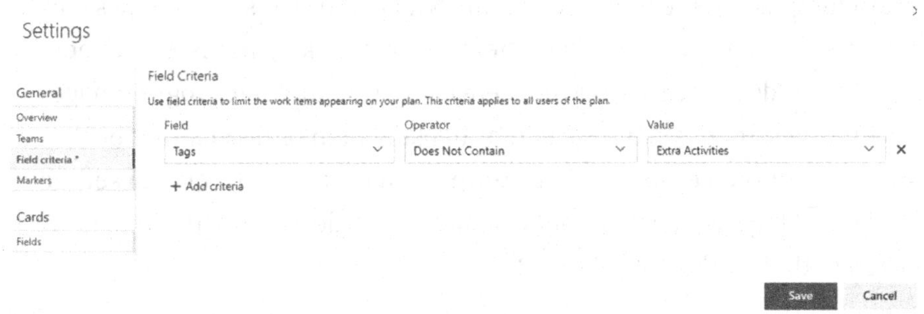

*Figure 3-5.  Field criteria in the Delivery Plan*

When you handle this supportive work, without having it visible to the default team, there is likely to be a discrepancy in capacity view if you share the same iteration information to the default/root team. To prevent this, set up the root team capacity to disregard the capacity allocated to the internal extra activities. For on-premise TFS, you can add a custom activity type by customizing the Task work item Activity field, similar to steps described for customizing pick list fields (`https://docs.microsoft.com/en-us/vsts/work/customize/add-modify-field#picklist`). This adds new activity types to capacity in iterations. For VSTS, you cannot add custom activity types as of the writing of this book.

# Handling Impediments/Roadblocks

The work that requires external support and the work that does not need to track with team activities—such as following up on the purchase of a development tool or SDK, getting a server environment, fixing a failing development machine, or even preparing a document for some purpose to support the team—should also be tracked somewhere.

VSTS/TFS has the Impediment/Issue work item type (Impediment in Scrum template, Issue in the CMMI and Agile templates) that allows you to track such activities and relate them to your backlog items if you need to (https://docs.microsoft.com/en-us/vsts/work/backlogs/manage-issues-impediments). If a particular backlog item or task cannot be executed without getting the issue/impediment resolved, you can set the task or backlog item back to the New state and add an Impediment/Issue related to that work item (Figure 3-6).

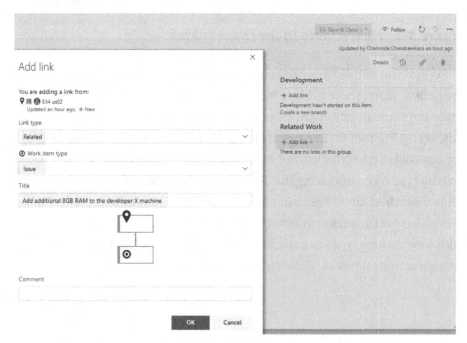

***Figure 3-6.*** *Adding an Issue to a work item*

# Working with Code

How to do development work, such as version controlling source code, branching strategies for source code repositories, and so on is not in the scope of this book. But for the sake of completeness, let's look at few areas where you can help your team.

If your team decides to work with the Git version control of TFS, it is a good practice to have a proper branching strategy. It is a good idea to have a branch for each backlog item and get it merged to development or the master branch via a pull request. You also have the option of creating a code branch from your backlog items as shown in Figure 3-7, which will be useful to your team. Again, do not interfere too much with these areas; rather, empower your technical team to make the required decisions, and let them keep on improving how they want to handle the development aspects.

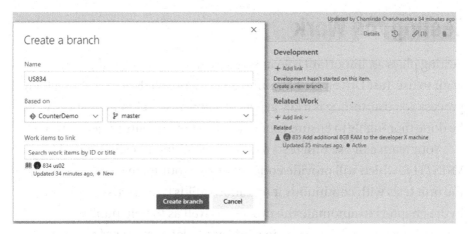

***Figure 3-7.*** *A branch of a backlog item*

Your team should always associate the work items with the commits/check-ins they make, regardless of whether they use TFVC (Team Foundation Version Control) or Git. You can ask the team to follow instructions in `https://docs.microsoft.com/en-us/vsts/work/track/link-work-items-support-traceability#link-work-items-code-artifacts-and-builds`.

You should encourage your team to use the code review features of VSTS/TFS to allow them to have good coding standards. If TFVC is used, your team can follow the instructions at `https://docs.microsoft.com/en-us/vsts/tfvc/get-code-reviewed-vs`, and if Git code is used, you can review it with pull requests (`https://docs.microsoft.com/en-us/vsts/git/pull-requests`).

Additionally, your team can utilize tools such as SonarQube and Veracode to create quality and secure code, which we discuss later in the chapter.

# Testing the Work

Testing plays an important role in software development and you may want to use Test Driven Development (TDD) as well. Regardless of which process you use, testing is a key aspect of software development and should be done thoroughly to ensure your team delivers a quality project/product.

Your team can use unit tests to start development testing, aided by VSTS/TFS, which will provide code coverage. Your team can then integrate the unit tests with continuous integration builds (we discuss this later in the chapter) to automate the process as well as to help publish code coverage results the team can view (`https://docs.microsoft.com/en-us/vsts/build-release/tasks/test/publish-code-coverage-results`). The extension in Visual Studio Marketplace comes with a dashboard widget for code coverage with a build (`https://marketplace.visualstudio.com/items?itemName=shanebdavis.code-coverage-dashboard-widgets`). We discuss dashboards later in this chapter.

It is possible to create test plans and test suites to organize the test cases your team develops related to backlog items. Your team can create static test suites, requirement-based test suites, and query-based test suites to organize the test plans. You can find a lot of useful information on this at `https://docs.microsoft.com/en-us/vsts/manual-test/reference-qa`. Your team can track test status as explained here: `https://docs.microsoft.com/en-us/vsts/manual-test/getting-started/track-test-status`. When a test plan is executed, you can view the outcome graphically in the Test Runs tab of VSTS/TFS, as shown in Figure 3-8.

***Figure 3-8.***   *Test outcome*

In addition to basic manual testing (`https://docs.microsoft.com/en-us/vsts/manual-test/getting-started/run-manual-tests`), it is possible to execute exploratory testing. Exploratory testing allows the team to explore the product/project backlog item implementation without having a test case, and the team can generate the test case depending on the steps they execute (Figure 3-9). As with normal manual testing, it is possible to create bugs related to the backlog item while executing the test. But the team can later modify a recorded test case to add more infromation to the test case or clear any unwanted steps generated while auto generating the test case, by altering and/or adding required additional steps. Your team can also use the Test and Feedback extension we discussed in Chapter 2 to execute exploratory testing (`https://docs.microsoft.com/en-us/vsts/manual-test/getting-started/perform-exploratory-tests`).

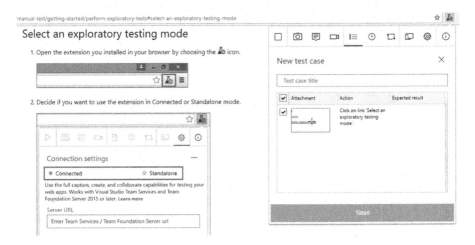

***Figure 3-9.***  *Creating a test case with exploratory testing*

# Monitoring the Progress

The team should monitor their progress and you should facilitate them to identify any threats to achieving the sprint target and to overcome them. It is really valuable to detect problems as soon as possible and to take corrective actions so that the delivery of committed items in the backlog can be fulfilled. Let's look at each one of the monitoring options.

- *Burndown:* A burndown chart shows how your team progress with the work by showing the remaining work getting reduced generally as the iteration progress graphically. In Chapter 2, we discussed using a story point burndown chart to identify the team progress in the iteration. Remember that even though you can use burndown with hour estimations on tasks, doing so is time-consuming, and there is no real benefit to looking at hours as long as the team does not deliver 100 percent of the backlog items. A story point burndown, on the other hand, can indicate more effectively the total story points in the current iteration and how the team is getting them done. If more and more story points are getting added due to the discovery of bugs within the iteration, or due to more backlog items getting added (we discuss this later in the chapter), burnup will happen instead of burndown.

- *Backlog Capacity View:* We discussed capacity in Chapter 2; Figure 3-10 indicates that in this instance, overall team capacity would not be enough, even though some activity types have enough team capacity. These very early indications help the team take corrective actions sooner than later.

*Figure 3-10.* *Capacity on iteration backlog view*

- *Task Board and Backlog Board:* The team should always look at these two boards and, as discussed previously, the styles on the cards on the board will help the team recognize the bottlenecks or any items that require the team's attention. Focusing on boards helps the team limit the work in progress and attend to the backlog from top to bottom. The team can take necessary corrective actions based on the indications it sees on these boards.

- *Velocity Chart:* The velocity chart helps to explain the team's capability of achieving story points/size/effort on backlog items. When you run a couple of sprints, you can identify the average velocity of the team. This information helps the team and you to forecast future work (we discuss forecasting future work in Chapter 4).

- *Cumulative Flow Diagram:* This diagram shows the progress from the perspective of all the iterations, from a defined time period up to the present. The cumulative flow diagram (Figure 3-11) also indicates the work in progress and the rate at which work items are getting completed vs. the rate at which items are getting added to the team project. In addition to the cumulative flow chart that is available by default in the backlog view, a more configurable widget is available in VSTS. You can view more details on cumulative flow at `https://docs.microsoft.com/en-us/vsts/report/dashboards/cumulative-flow`.

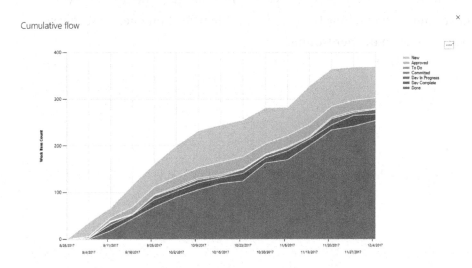

***Figure 3-11.*** *The cumulative flow diagram*

- *Queries, Charts, and Dashboards:* You can write custom queries and create charts and dashboards, which we discuss in the section "Visualizing and Positively Impacting the Team," later in this chapter.

- *Build Deployments, and Test Outcomes:* Teams can create dashboard widgets, charts, and so on to monitor the builds, deployments, and test outcomes, which we discuss further in "Visualizing and Positively Impacting the Team."

# Avoiding Defects

Defects/bugs in software are costly and can even affect your team's reputation with clients. The cost defect increases as it reaches each stage in a software delivery lifecycle, and bugs found in production can even cost you your project, as shown in Figure 3-12. A simple bug that is miscalculating interest on savings accounts in a banking application or interest provisioning process can cost millions of dollars, and your customer, or bank, may be in a big trouble with their clients; surely you will be in even deeper trouble.

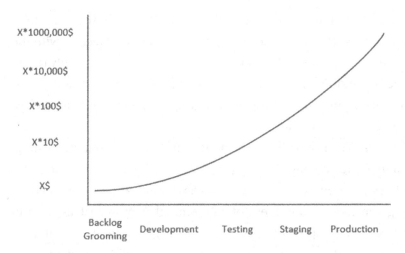

*Figure 3-12.* *The cost of a bug*

You can take many actions to identify bugs/defects as soon as possible. If your team performs good backlog grooming sessions and prepares test cases well before the iteration starts, they have a really good starting point from which to detect defects early. Fixing bugs detected at the backlog grooming level only costs your team a small amount of time and effort. The team might have to alter a few test cases and redefine some tasks and backlog item content, including acceptance criteria. Even if the team has to abandon a backlog item entirely and re-create new backlog items in agreement with the product owner, finding bugs early is not a big cost at all.

In the development stage of software, a lot of bugs may occur if your team did not follow certain good practices. Code review is one such good practice that your team can follow, as we discussed earlier. Sometimes it is better to use two minds rather than one to get a component implemented. You can do this by introducing pair programming when it makes sense to do so. An article at www.ppig.org/papers/17th-chong.pdf provides you with more insight on when and how pair programming works. We mentioned already that sometimes the QA members of the team are idle at the start of iterations and have a bit of time when they can help the developers. That help can come in the form of pair testing with the developers. At any time of the iteration, if the developer is ready to show what he is working on, the tester can sit with him at his developer machine and test the application. This way your team can identify issues well before they reach the testing stage.

Your team will also test the backlog items developed in the testing stage and fixing any bugs they detect. Once the first set of backlog items completes development, your team starts developing the next set of backlog items. The team does not have enough time to test all the backlog items developed in previous iterations in any given iteration. But it is risky to release the project/product to production without testing each and every component. Manually doing this sort of regression is not feasible. Therefore, your team can introduce test automation to reduce the size of the team needed for regressions. The ideal solution would be to run a daily smoke test suite on your solutions and deploy nightly to the testing environment. We discuss VSTS/TFS options to implement such automation later in the chapter. The work done by the team for automation can also be tracked with the supportive work tracking strategy that we discussed in a previous section of this chapter.

Your team should test the applications they develop for load and performance under stress. This gives the team the opportunity to detect performance issues and fix them early, otherwise, these may be encountered in the production a few months after the release. VSTS/TFS with Visual Studio offers many options to perform load and performance tests as described at `https://docs.microsoft.com/en-us/vsts/load-test/`.

You should keep your staging environment set up similar to your production environment. This allows the team to find bugs that could occur in production well before they actually reach production.

Your team should also make sure that each deployment to the testing or staging environment happens in exactly the same way as it would happen in production. For this to work, before they deploy to testing/staging, the team should make the a replica equivalent to the production-deployed version of the product's testing/staging environment. This means that if any additional deployment on top of the production version has happened in these environments, it should be reverted to the production version before each deployment happens. Infrastructure as code and automated deployment tools with VSTS/TFS will help your team achieve this goal. When you perform deployments in this way, you are assured that production will not fail due to deployment issues.

Identifying the cause of defects in the production environment is a most difficult activity, but many modern tools can help you with this. One such tool is Application Insights (`https://azure.microsoft.com/en-us/resources/videos/application-insights-how-to-detect-issues-solve-problems-and-continuously-improve-your-web-applicati/`).

# Facilitating Unavoidable Changes

The unforeseen can happen at any time in life, and in software development this is no different. For instance, you may discover a bug in your current iteration development that requires the team to go back to the drawing board and think things through from the beginning. Or the team may find a large, unfixable bug within the iteration just as you are almost at the end of it. You may have to give up a backlog item as a result. Your product owner/customer may demand that you take a new backlog item into the sprint. She may say that without it, she will not accept the iteration. Or perhaps a sudden critical bug will surface in production that needs the whole team's attention to fix.

No matter how these types of requirements arise, you must help the team handle them in a graceful manner. For example, if you must take a new backlog item into the current iteration, negotiate with the product owner to take out one or more items from the bottom of the iteration backlog to accommodate the incoming item. Make sure to discuss the issue with the team and get their technical opinion so you can constructively communicate with all the stakeholders, including the product owner, and come to an agreement that everyone is willing to accept. Facilitating necessary discussions with technical leadership and business owners is key to your success managing these situations. You can use VSTS/TFS boards and other progress monitoring options we discussed earlier to give the current picture to every stakeholder and bring them all onto the same page. The discussion should focus on how everyone comes out of this situation instead of devolving into pointing figures at each other.

Certain cases might cause your current iteration work value to become null and void. In such cases, with the product owner's consent, it is possible to abandon an iteration. If this is done, all the remaining work should return to the backlog and be groomed, sized, and reprioritized before you start the next sprint. We discuss this more in Chapter 4.

# Handling Disaster Situations

Another challenge in supporting an Agile team is handling disaster situations. Disaster can come in many forms, for example,

- Your key team members may fall sick during a critical time.

- Your developer or testing environment hardware may fail suddenly.

- A natural disaster may interfere with your team members' ability to carry out their duties.

- Your team may discover a technical design failure in
  the project that points to the necessity of a complete
  overhaul.

Regardless of the type of disaster, successful management of it relies heavily on facilitating collaborative and constructive discussion among all stakeholders. In a situation in which a team member cannot attend work for some reason, other team members will jump in and cover up for her if you set the right mood in the team as their facilitator. The team should always feel that you are there to back them up and that they can count on you. If you can cultivate the team's trust in each other and in you as their servant leader, the team will be able to come out of any situation, miraculously. It is this team spirit, mutual trust, and collaboration that makes teams succeed.

Accountability for team members' or a team's action and visibility are also important aspects of team building. VSTS/TFS provides visibility in all actions of the team, which allows team members to be responsible for their actions. As their facilitator, you should always support them to overcome any mistakes they make by helping individual team members and by letting other team members help, rather than by using accusations, by pointing fingers, or by placing blame on the team or an individual. Even though VSTS/TFS provides visibility, sometimes you need to keep certain problems within the team and manage them yourself rather than escalating everything to higher management for punishment and control purposes.

Always discuss the disaster situation with the team, and lay out a plan together; only then should you present it to stakeholders (product owner, higher management of the company) alone (without the team) and get their buy-in for the plan. Keep supporting and facilitating the team and be with them to overcome the situation. No matter what tool you use, success lies in how you build trust and relationships within your team. After all, people and relationships are more important than the tools and processes.

# Release Stability

To succeed in agility in software delivery, your team needs to release rapidly to the testing environments. Some Agile teams even go to the level of releasing to the test environment nightly and releasing to production at the end of each iteration. A good example of this is a VSTS team releasing on a three-week-release cadence.

To make releases often, automation is a must. If your team is only deploying manually, it will be impossible to do a couple of releases a week, and forget about releasing nightly as it is impossible to do this manually.

A package should always be built once and should be deployed to each target environment, with an approved workflow as depicted in Figure 3-13. Each stage should be reverted to the production version before getting deployed with the new version to assure production deployment stability.

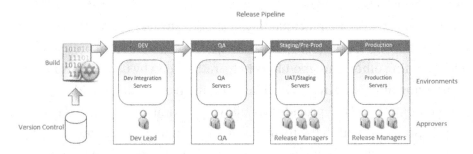

***Figure 3-13.*** *The release pipeline*

Your team can implement infrastructure deployment with code as well. VSTS/TFS has a comprehensive set of features and many free marketplace extensions to manage builds and deployments. You can set up test automation after deployment to any target environment so it executes smoke or regression tests on the deployed software. This helps the team automatically validate the previously implemented functionality before they begin testing on new functionalities. As we discussed earlier, make sure you keep the backlog items associated with the code submissions to enable automated release notes with the deployments.

To learn all the basics you and your team need to implement successful build release pipelines, including test automation, refer to Chaminda Chandrasekara's *Beginning Build and Release Management with TFS 2017 and VSTS*, available at `https://www.apress.com/in/book/9781484228104` (Chapter 11 of the build release management book discusses automating release notes [as shown here in Figure 3-14] based on deploying the target environment). New unified agent–based test automation capabilities are described at `https://docs.microsoft.com/en-us/vsts/build-release/test/run-automated-tests-from-test-hub`.

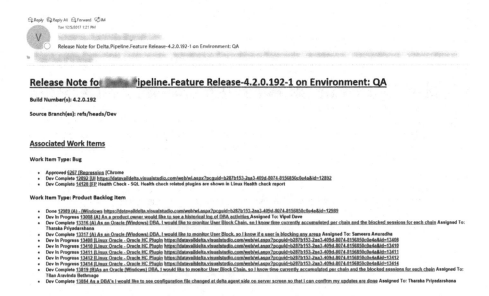

***Figure 3-14.*** *An automated release note*

Even if your team deploys to certain environments manually, they must prepare a checklist to make sure they are not going to miss any step of the deployment. However, we recommend you use automation for deployments as much as possible since it is more systematic, efficient, and reliable.

Another important aspect of making your release stable is making the developed software code high quality and secure. To improve the code quality, you can review the code as we discussed earlier. In addition, you can analyze the code with tools such as SonarQube to measure its quality. When integrated with VSTS/TFS builds, SonarQube can alert your team to the quality gate status after analyzing the code in various aspects. Even a build can be configured to fail if the quality gate fails, as shown in Figure 3-15.

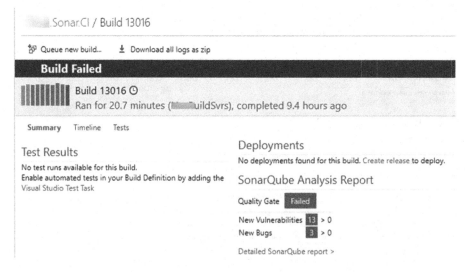

***Figure 3-15.*** *Build failing due to quality gate failure*

The build provides a link to access detail information of the analysis performed, on the SonarQube server with a lot of drill-down capability so you can further analyze the reasons for the quality gate status (Figure 3-16). Your team can learn how to set up SonarQube for VSTS/TFS builds at `http://chamindac.blogspot.com/2017/02/sonarqube-extension-for-vststfs.html`.

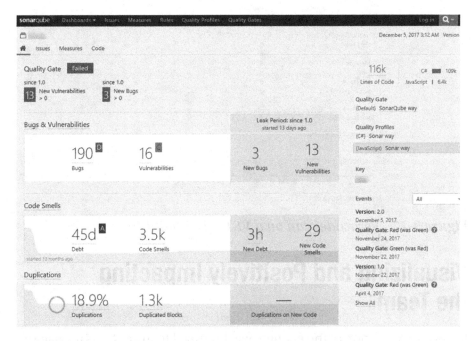

***Figure 3-16.*** *The SonarQube project dashboard*

You can also use the Veracode (not free) platform to analyze the security aspects of the code with VSTS/TFS builds (Figure 3-17). An extension is available in the Visual Studio Marketplace (`https://marketplace.visualstudio.com/items?itemName=Veracode.veracode-vsts-build-extension`) that you can use to upload your binaries and trigger a Veracode scan.

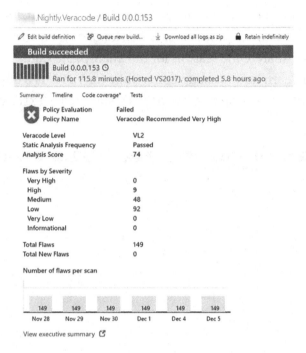

*Figure 3-17.* *Veracode scan on a VSTS/TFS build*

# Visualizing and Positively Impacting the Team

In a previous section of the chapter, we discussed many options available in VSTS/TFS that you can use to monitor the progress of your team. Let's look at how queries and dashboards can help you visualize the status of the project in different aspects.

You can write different queries (https://docs.microsoft.com/en-us/vsts/work/track/using-queries) to filter your work items in various ways. You have the ability to create trend charts (https://docs.microsoft.com/en-us/vsts/report/dashboards/charts) using those queries and then add them to the default dashboard (https://docs.microsoft.com/en-us/vsts/report/dashboards/add-charts-to-dashboard), or create your own dashboards in VSTS/TFS (https://docs.microsoft.com/en-us/vsts/report/dashboards/dashboards) as shown in Figure 3-18.

***Figure 3-18.***   *A dashboard with charts*

You can include build, deployment-related charts, and test results, including test automation results, in dashboards. VSTS supports Analytics widgets in dashboards to allow for further visualizing capability with the Cumulative Flow Diagram (CFD), Velocity, Lead Time, Cycle Time, Burndown, and Burnup widgets (https://docs.microsoft.com/en-us/vsts/report/analytics/analytics-widgets-vsts). All these visualizations will help you and your team identify any issues and take corrective actions.

Bombarded with the overwhelming availability of data on the progress of your team, at times, you might make wrong choices. Such choices sometimes cause chaos in projects. For instance, if you are looking at the burndown on the last day of the iteration, and you tell the team it has done an awful job, the members are apt to be demotivated, which will lead to the team giving up on everything.

But how can you make sure you positively impact the team? First, remember that you should be the facilitator or enabler. You should provide support to help your team understand and practice Agile/Scrum. You should help the team focus on team goals rather than individual goals. You must always energetically look for process improvements and guide the team to adopt such improvements in an enjoyable way.

You must also play the role of negotiator, especially between the team and the product owner. You must effectively communicate with both parties and ensure collaboration between them. Your job is to bridge the gap between your team and the client's business. Your responsibility is to work closely with the product owner to identify business challenges and also support the team to accommodate business requirements in an effective way.

You should positively influence your team *and* the business team and have the ability to set reasonable expectations in the product owner, by negotiating and influencing him, if he is highly demanding. You can use the visualization capability of VSTS/TFS to create the background required for such negotiations.

You should also be the protector of the team, by shielding them from interferences and impediments, and you should keep their focus on the sprint goal. You must strike a balance when protecting the team, however, as you must also keep in mind the business's interests. Be resourceful so you can creatively remove impediments from the team.

Conflict resolution also plays an important part in your role. You must earn everyone's trust and respect. If conflicts are positively impacting the work, such as various opinions on technology implementations, encourage the team to have such conflicts and resolve them constructively to improve the quality of work. This is also true with challenges that are geared toward improving the process. But if the conflicts are rising between team members due to personal issues, make sure these are fixed immediately as political conflicts within an Agile team spell disaster.

Another of your responsibilities is building your team. It is important for you to accept your team's smaller failures since lessons learned from failure are often worth more than the advice you give before failure. Lower the bar when necessary and celebrate small, regular successes in the team. This positive momentum will help you raise the bar later and celebrate much higher success stories with your team. Happiness in the working environment is important to making your team succeed, so help your team enjoy life while they work hard for the team goals.

You should be disruptive when you need to be and be sure to show empathy for the people around you. Do not be afraid to break the rules and make changes. Your willingness to experiment and go ahead with continuous improvements will surely influence your team to strive for success. Maybe introducing a mid-sprint review to get feedback from the product owner will be helpful, or perhaps you can conduct this type of review within the team to check on the team's progress. However, avoid micromanaging at all costs; trusting your team and earning their trust is a vital part of your role, no matter what tools you use or how capable your tools are in implementing Agile practices.

You can use VSTS/TFS visualization capabilities to build awareness in the team; they should think about where they are heading and when they need to take necessary corrective actions. You can influence your team by showing the team's progress visually and by parsing the team for success, so that the team keeps on updating work items as the members progress with work. Correctly representing status is important for the team, and team members should understand the value of this by experiencing the benefits of the correct status visibility. Let the team members be innovative with the VSTS/TFS tool and help them come up with creative solutions to the challenges they face. Creating automated steps as often as you can, such as automating the task estimation as we discussed in Chapter 2, is productive as well as effective to the productivity of the team.

# Summary

In this chapter, we focused on daily activity and positively working with iteration goals, while effectively using VSTS/TFS as a tool. You learned the importance of performing backlog grooming activities, while working on the current iteration in order to make the requirements ready for the next iterations. We discussed several challenges an Agile team may face and how you can act as a successful servant leader to overcome them, using tools as well as other traits that you should cultivate. We also highlighted the importance of the cultural impact on an Agile team's success.

In the next chapter, we explore how we should come to the end of an iteration and set the background to start the next iteration. We then discuss in more detail what steps you need to followed to make continuous improvements to the team in the coming iterations.

# CHAPTER 4

# Work After an Iteration

In previous chapters, you learned about the things that you need to set up before you and your team can start working on an iteration and how you can effectively execute an iteration using VSTS/TFS as a tool. In previous chapters, we also described challenges you will face in the initial planning and execution of the iteration and how you can use VSTS/TFS capabilities effectively to overcome them. However, be aware that the features and information availability in VSTS/TFS may lead you to circumstances in which micromanagement may creep in and disrupt the purpose of building agility in your team; we also discussed such pitfalls in previous chapters to make you cautious and aware of these and to prevent you from falling into them. With this knowledge, you can build empowered teams and practice Agile using VSTS/TFS as a helpful tool, rather than one that misleads your processes and practices.

In this chapter, we go through post-iteration activities and steps you need to perform to get getting ready for the next iteration. First, it is important to review the completed work from the previous iteration and make sure you and your team understand how to handle partially completed work before you move onto the next iteration. Discussing challenges faced by the team in previous iteration helps the team make improvements to how they will work in coming iteration. In this chapter we discuss in detail how to pick items for the next iteration and what you should avoid during post-iteration activities and planning for the next iteration to be an effective Agile team. Our objective here is to explore the

© Chaminda Chandrasekara, Sanjaya Yapa 2018
C. Chandrasekara and S. Yapa, *Effective Team Management with VSTS and TFS*,
https://doi.org/10.1007/978-1-4842-3558-4_4

Analytics widgets in VSTS that allow you determine the lead times, the cycle times, and the forecasting capabilities of the work that your team would deliver in the future iterations, and to help you plan your releases in a predictable way.

# Review

As we discussed in Chapter 2, each user story or bug fix should meet the definition of done (DoD) in order for it to be released to the client environments. A shippable increment of software expected at the end of an Agile/Scrum iteration should comprise backlog items (stories) and/or bug fixes that are fully developed and tested and that can be deployed to production environments, but only if the client is happy with the implementation.

You should only select the 100-percent developed and tested stories and fixes while making sure you avoid including partially finished work in the version that you release after the iteration. Skipping the partially done work is a challenge in the release increment if proper branching and/or architectural patterns are not followed by the team. Even though discussing how to define software architecture so it supports the capability to switch features on and off in a release is out of scope of the book, it is an important aspect your team should consider when implementing software.

In such scenarios, feature toggles will save the day. A *feature toggle* is a feature switch or flipper that helps you keep your production code in sync with the development version. This is extremely useful in scenarios in which the end users are not ready for the new feature. For more details about feature toggles, check this out: `https://dev.to/samueleresca/continuos-delivery-using-feature-toggle`.

By the end of the iteration, your team should have DoD-met stories and bug fixes deployed to the preproduction environment, but only after they have been fully tested in previous stages such as development integration, quality assurance (QA), user acceptance testing (UAT), and so on. As per Agile/Scrum practices, teams should demonstrate each of their completed features in the sprint review meeting to the client/product owner to get final approval before deploying them to production. If the demonstration is done in a preproduction environment, the validity and reliability of the software increment becomes higher as it is much closer to the production implementation.

Product owners may or may not approve the release to production, but such releases that are not approved should not be considered total failures of implementation as long as the team understands what needs to be fixed and accepted DoD criteria are met for each feature. In cases in which there is a gap between the team's understanding of DoD and the product owner's, discussion of how to improve the way the criteria for DoD is defined should ensue; we discuss this later in this chapter. Some teams follow a different release cadence from iteration length and have multiple iterations before a release to production happens. Even in such situations, it is worth demonstrating the completed features at the end of each iteration, as this gives the team an opportunity to get early feedback on implementation, and this satisfies the Agile thinking of *fail fast, fail often*. This phrase should not be misunderstood as invitation to fail or an encouragement of failure. Rather, fail fast, fail often allows your teams to learn fast and fix issues sooner rather than later, which keeps the cost of fixes lower, because the cost is much higher when bugs are detected and need to be fixed toward the end of project, or in production, as we discussed in the Chapter 3. To understand more about fail fast, fail often in the context of success, take a look at www.arrkgroup.com/thought-leadership/fail-fast-fail-often-explained/.

Once the review session with the product owner/client is done, the owner/client can start providing feedback on the implementation of the iteration. This can happen as voluntary feedback or the team can request feedback for individual implemented features and get the feedback as we discussed in Chapter 2.

# Handling Partially Done Stories

If work is not 100-percent complete, the features it contains cannot be included in the increment that is shipping at the end of the iteration, since partially done work cannot generate value to the client business process to improve it. The completed portion of the work should remain in the iteration that just ended, and any in-progress tasks and not-yet-started tasks of a story or a bug fix should be taken back to the backlog. Some teams do this incorrectly by moving the incomplete work directly to the next iteration; this should be avoided because the partially completed work should be evaluated, reprioritized, and re-estimated before the decision is made to work on them in the next iteration. This is because priorities might have changed in the project, so other work may now need to be given higher priority than the partially completed work from the previous iteration.

# Moving Partially Completed Work to the Backlog

You can move the user story/product backlog item (PBI) or a bug work item to the backlog by changing its iteration path to the backlog iteration path. Then you have to move all child tasks that are in progress or new to the backlog by changing their iteration paths to the backlog iteration path. Instead of changing each work item manually, simply drag and drop the story/PBI or bug work item to the backlog, which automatically moves the child tasks that are not closed back to the backlog. Closed child tasks remain in the iteration since the work for them was already completed in the iteration, as we discussed earlier. If you need to, you can drag and drop multiple stories and bugs by highlighting them and dragging (Figure 4-1).

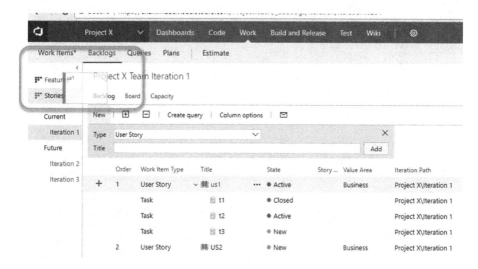

***Figure 4-1.*** *Drag and drop the story to the backlog*

Instead of dragging and dropping after you highlight required work items, you can right-click to access the menu, click Move to Iteration, and then click the Backlog menu option to move them to the backlog with the child tasks that are not closed (Figure 4-2).

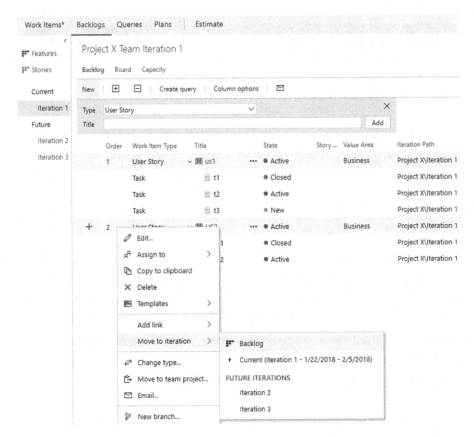

***Figure 4-2.*** *Moving stories to the backlog using the menu*

When you move the parent work items to the backlog by dragging and dropping or using the menu, the closed task work items remain in the iteration; the parent work item remains visible inside the iteration even though it has been moved to the backlog. This behavior correctly represents the partially done work (tasks completed) for a story or a bug in a given iteration. Figure 4-3 illustrates completed tasks that remain in the iteration with a the user story has been moved to the backlog.

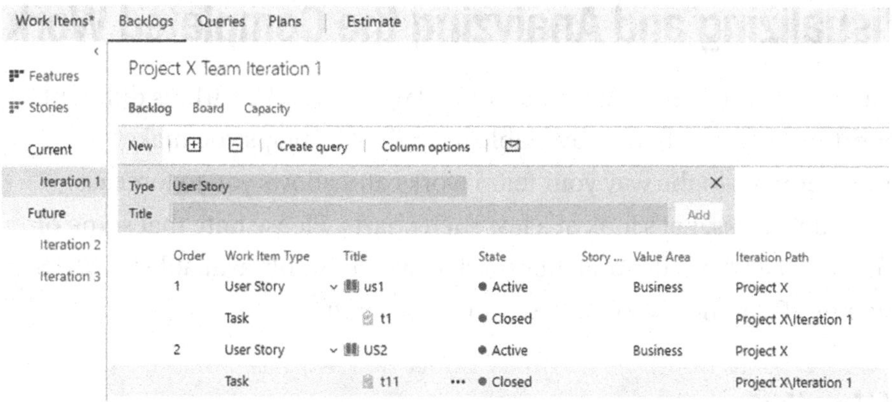

*Figure 4-3.* *Completed tasks remains in the iteration*

Once moved to the backlog, the story/PBI or bug work items should be re-estimated after the remaining effort is evaluated. There may have been changes to acceptance criteria or even requirement changes to these items. In the planning session for the next sprint, discuss and select these work items depending on their priority and the priority of other work items. In other words, once moved back to the backlog, all these items are considered similarly to other backlog items, and they go through the same process to get selected for the next or any future iteration. You can even have a backlog grooming session between the iterations to evaluate these work items compared to other work items that are already prioritized and groomed in the backlog. We discuss this more later in the chapter when we go through the process of planning the next iteration.

# Visualizing and Analyzing the Completed Work

Visualizing and analyzing the completed work with the various different reports and charts that are available in VSTS/TFS helps you make improvements to the way your team works and allows you to forecast future deliveries. Let's look at a few such charts. Please note that some of them are based on the Analytics service, which is only available for VSTS and not TFS at the time of the writing of this book.

## Velocity

Fully completed and DoD met stories and fixes, accumulated size gives the velocity of the iteration that is completed. In VSTS/TFS, the velocity chart provides information about completed sizes (achieved story points) of iterations as well as in-progress sizes. It is arguable whether team velocity for a completed iteration should consider in-progress velocity or not. But in reality, in-progress work adds no value to the customer, and considering it as team velocity has no validity. For example, as shown in Figure 4-4, Sprint – 2017.32 is a completed iteration and it has a DoD-met velocity of 135 points, whereas 14 points are in progress, so the actual team velocity for the iteration is 135 points.

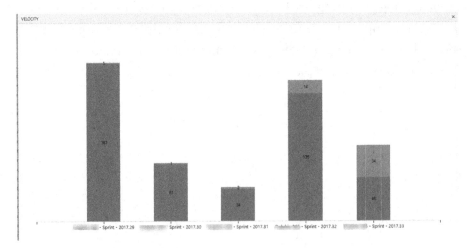

***Figure 4-4.*** *The velocity chart*

VSTS provides an additional widget to identify and provide more information on the velocity of the team. To get this widget, you need to install the Analytics extension to VSTS from VSTS Marketplace. Once the extension is installed, you can set up the Velocity widget in the dashboard (we discussed dashboards in Chapter 3) of the team. This Velocity widget provides you with achieved velocity vs. planned velocity, and work completed late also can be identified (Figure 4-5). More information on this Velocity widget can be found at `https://docs.microsoft.com/en-us/vsts/report/dashboards/team-velocity`.

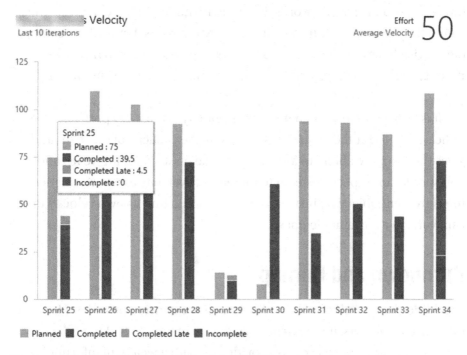

***Figure 4-5.*** *The Velocity widget in VSTS*

Using each iteration velocity, you should calculate an average velocity for the team; do this manually because VSTS/TFS does not provide an average velocity calculation automatically at the time of the writing of this book. The following is the formula for this:

*Average Velocity = Accumulated Velocity in All Iterations/ No. of Iterations*

If you are using the Scrum process template for on-premises TFS with SQL Server Reporting Services (SSRS), you get a velocity report that provides an average velocity line that is useful for forecasting work for future iterations. In other words, if your team has completed a few sprints, your ability to forecast future sprints greatly improves. For further reading, please visit `https://docs.microsoft.com/en-us/vsts/report/sql-reports/velocity?view=vsts`. We discuss this topic more later in this chapter.

It is important to keep in mind that velocity is not a key performance indicator (KPI) for the team. It just provides the capacity of the team and gives the team the ability to forecast and take on work for future iterations. You should not expect the team to increase its velocity as a performance measurement objective; instead the team should find its own velocity that can work on a sustainable phase.

# Burndown and Burnup

In addition to the velocity chart, the Analytics extension provides a few other useful widgets. Just search for Analytics in the VSTS Marketplace. Burndown and Burnup widgets provide you with a wealth of information on how your team is progressing. You can learn more about these widgets at `https://docs.microsoft.com/en-us/vsts/report/dashboards/configure-burndown-burnup-widgets`. It is important to configure these charts per your team requirements and understand the meaning of each of the values and lines shown. The information provided in

`https://docs.microsoft.com/en-us/vsts/report/dashboards/`
`configure-burndown-burnup-widgets#interpret-a-burndown-or-`
`burnup-widget-chart` provides a comprehensive overview of the
interpretation of these charts; the following is a summary of the most
critical points:

- *Total Scope:* The scope change of the project is
  represented by the line that considers the completed
  work as well. Figure 4-6 shows a significant increase in
  scope.

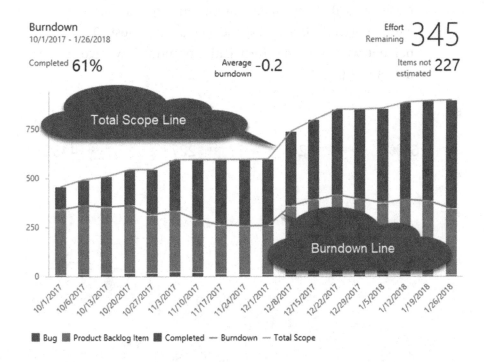

*Figure 4-6.* *The burndown line*

- *Burndown:* The burndown line plotted in the chart shows how fast your team gets the work completed. In Figure 4-6, the average burndown shows as a negative value because the burndown rate has decreased as an average due to an increase in the remaining work, probably due to the significant scope increase in the project.

- *Burnup:* If the burnup chart is analyzed for the same time period (see Figure 4-7), it provides another view of how the work is progressing. Even though the scope has increased, the team has completed a significant amount of work. The total scope increase is almost 50 percent, which justifies the negative burndown average in Figure 4-6.

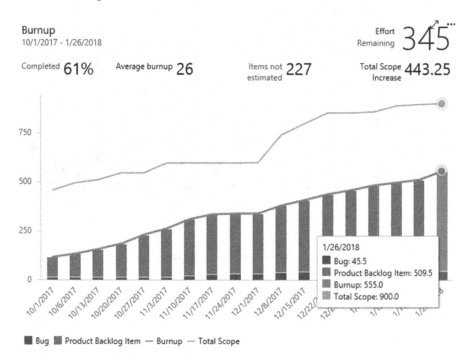

*Figure 4-7.* *The burnup chart*

# Lead Time and Cycle Time

Identifying the lead time and cycle time of your team helps you determine how long it takes for work to go through development and testing to get completed.

- *Lead Time:* The total time it takes to complete the work item starting at the time it was created

- *Cycle Time:* The time it takes to complete the work item starting at the time the active work began

The Analytics extensions displayed in Figure 4-8 are available in the VSTS Marketplace, which we discussed in previous section. To learn how to configure the extension, go to `https://docs.microsoft.com/en-us/vsts/report/dashboards/cycle-time-and-lead-time`.

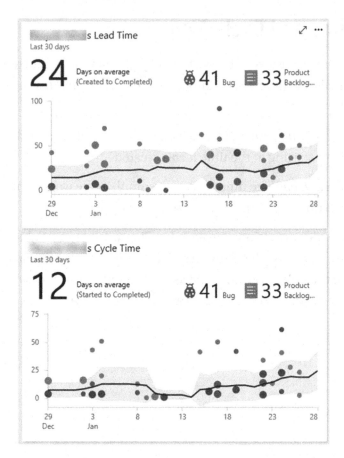

*Figure 4-8.* *Lead time and cycle time*

# Cumulative Flow

In addition to the default cumulative flow chart available in the backlog view, a more configurable Cumulative Flow widget is available in the VSTS, which you can enable by installing the Analytics extension from the VSTS Marketplace. In this Cumulative Flow widget, illustrated in Figure 4-9, you can set up which backlog level you should consider for cumulative flow, whereas the default available chart considers all the work items available to the team.

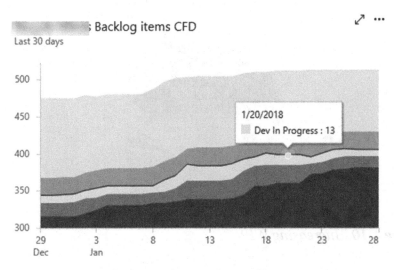

**Figure 4-9.** *The backlog items' cumulative flow*

Understanding the patterns of cumulative flow helps you identify the answers to a few questions and you can then use those to make decisions to take necessary corrective actions.

## Understanding How the Work Is Progressing

When you use the Analytics extension, you can filter the backlog for the Cumulative Flow widget. Work in progress should have mostly thin parallel lines, while the last column should increase in size gradually. If a widening gap appears in the work in progress (WIP), as shown in Figure 4-10, work is not getting completed and the team is working on too many items in parallel, which is not a good sign. The team should take action to complete work together as a team without starting on other new work.

***Figure 4-10.*** *Increasing WIP*

## Bulges in Cumulative Flow

When some portion of work is not getting completed as expected, bulges may occur in the cumulative flow (Figure 4-11). For example, a bulge may occur in the development-completed state if testing work is happening slowly and development work is getting completed more quickly. Normally a bulge indicates an issue in the next stage (state) of the process rather than in the state in which the bulge is shown. In this example scenario, you could support your testing members of the team with the development members who are also participating in testing activity. This is a major reason why crossfunctional and multiskilled teams are valuable in Agile practices.

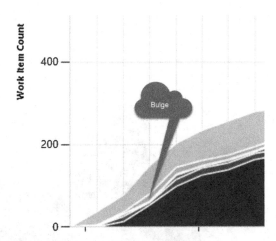

*Figure 4-11.* *A Bulge in the cumulative flow*

## Flat Lines and Scope Changes

A flat line in the cumulative flow diagram (CFD) may occur when the team takes more time than planned to get work moved from one process state to another. This could be because the team has not updated the work items regularly, which may have caused the flat lines. A similar effect can happen even in burndown and burnup charts if the team does not update work items regularly. Always encourage the team to drag the work items to the relevant column in the Kanban boards, and use the daily scrum meeting to check that and identify if the work item is in the right column. Flat lines occur when multiple process states do not progress as planned, and if one state progresses while the other does not, then a bulge, as explained in previous section, may occur.

Scope changes are also visible (Figure 4-12) when the initial state of the process is made available to the CFD. You can find details on configuring the Cumulative Flow widget at https://docs.microsoft.com/en-us/vsts/report/dashboards/cumulative-flow#configure-the-cfd-widget and the built-in cumulative flow chart at https://docs.microsoft.com/en-us/vsts/report/dashboards/cumulative-flow#configure-the-built-in-cumulative-flow-chart.

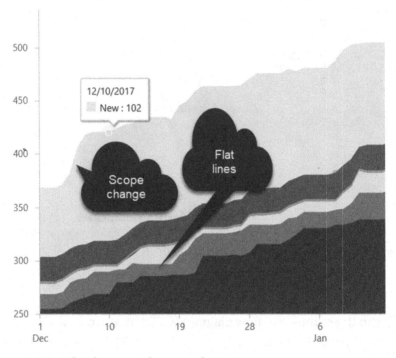

***Figure 4-12.*** *Flat lines and scope changes*

All of these charts and widgets provide you and the team with valuable information about how well your team is progressing with the work. It is important that you communicate the meaning of these charts to the team and explain how to interpret them. When the team understands what each change happening in these charts and widgets indicates, with your support, they can make quality decisions about necessary improvements in order to rapidly add value for your end users (clients).

# Planning the Next Iteration

We have already discussed the importance of conducting a review of previous 100-percent completed iteration work with the participation of client/product owner, of getting the in-progress work of the previous iteration back to the backlog, and of visualizing and understanding the completed work with the help of the charts and diagrams that are available in VSTS/TFS. None of the in-progress work should remain in the previous iteration; it should all be in the backlog before you plan your next sprint. In addition, no items should be selected for any of the future iterations at this stage. Some teams make the mistake of assigning work for a few iterations into future. This is a really bad practice because until you complete an iteration, you cannot know what will remain as in-progress work. Additionally, the priorities of your client business might change and the backlog may require reprioritization. So we strongly discourage you from assigning work for future iterations; in your sprint planning session, you should only assign work for the next immediate iteration if you really want to embrace agility. You may be wondering how to predict the releases when you have no work planned for future iterations. You can find the answer to this later in this chapter, when we discuss the forecasting capabilities of VSTS/TFS.

Another important factor for successful sprint planning for the next iteration is having a well-groomed and sized backlog by the end of a given sprint. Many teams lose focus of the backlog when they start working on an iteration, and as a result, they run into an imprecise set of backlog items, which need lots of clarifications, before they can size or add a definition of done (DoD). In simple terms, backlog items are not met with definition of ready (DoR), which we discussed in Chapter 2. To prevent this from happening, your team should invest a required amount of time on the backlog grooming activity during an iteration, as explained in Chapter 3.

With a DoR-met backlog—including the in-progress items from the previous iteration re-estimated and reprioritized—and considering the other backlog items that depend on the current business priorities of the project, your team should pick the topmost items of the backlog to assign to the next iteration. How many items your team picks should be based on the average velocity of the team. Let's now spend more time on this and the forecasting capabilities of VSTS/TFS.

# Forecasting Future Work

VSTS/TFS allows you to forecast work based on the average velocity so you can predict how many backlog items can be completed at the end of each future iteration. You can use On/Off forecasting and Show/Hide in-progress work to get the desired view. As we discussed earlier in the chapter, you need to calculate the average velocity of your team. When you have, place it in the "Forecasting based on velocity of" field, as shown in Figure 4-13. The forecasting lines are drawn based on this velocity value and the number of future iterations you have selected for the team. For more information on forecasting with VSTS/TFS refer to `https://docs.microsoft.com/en-us/vsts/work/scrum/forecast`.

Even though Figure 4-13 shows in-progress work assigned to an iteration, no items are assigned to an iteration since the figure was created in the middle of an iteration. At this point just before a sprint planning session, when you look at the forecast, you should have no items assigned to an iteration. However, you can use a forecasting tool at any point in time to get an idea of how many sprints you need to complete the backlog items or to find out how much work your team can complete by a given iteration.

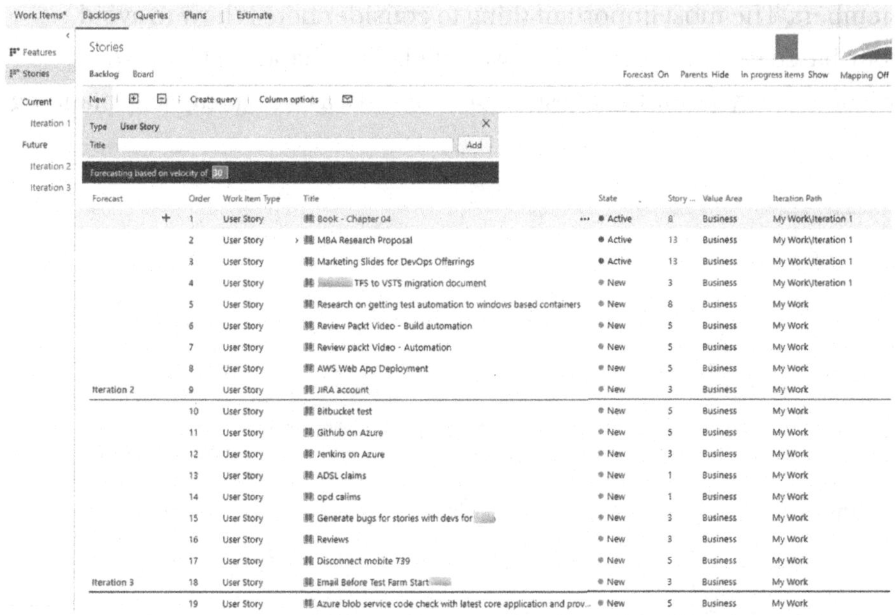

*Figure 4-13.* *Forecasting with VSTS/TFS*

The average-velocity-based forecast gives you a hint on how much of your backlog your team should pick up for the next iteration. Your team can just follow this hint or make its own decision on how many items to pick; for example, it is okay to be a bit overly ambitious or cautious when you are deciding the work item count for next iteration. It takes few iterations for the team to get into a rhythm and identify the sustainable velocity.

# Planning Capacity for the Next Iteration

You can easily copy over the capacity plan from the previous iteration by clicking the link to copy capacity from the previous iteration, as shown in Figure 4-14. You may also have to change the team off days and the individual off days after copying over the capacity, and you may need to alter whether any member of the team was reallocated or add new team

113

members. The most important thing to consider here is how to avoid hour-based capacity planning, as we detailed in Chapter 2. Doing so promotes story-point-based estimation for tasks as well as capacity planning.

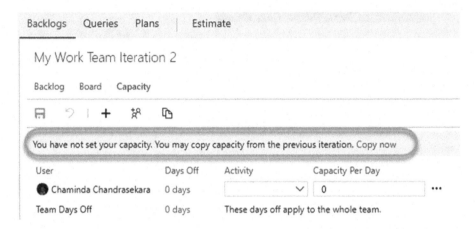

*Figure 4-14.*  *Copying capacity from the previous iteration*

# Continuous Improvement

At the end of each sprint/iteration, the team should discuss what can be improved in terms of workflow and how to avoid any unwanted problems the team encountered during the previous iteration. Most importantly, make sure to encourage each and every team member to contribute an idea to a list improvements. Once the team has made this list, it should discuss these items and prioritize them to identify the most critical improvements the team can make. It is important that the team picks only two or three items from the top of this prioritized list and creates an action plan as well as assigns responsibility to the team to make sure that the improvements are practiced and followed. As scrum master, you should guide the team to implement the suggestions and support the team members in identifying the most critical improvements required.

During this discussion, make sure to evaluate whether the team's previously taken actions on improvements are successfully implemented or not and the impact of those improvements. Sometimes these improvement attempts cause more problems to team productivity and agility, so this evaluation will help the team improve on previous improvements. In simple terms, there is no best solution—there is always a better solution than the previous one, however, and the solutions will keep on improving. Making the team believe in continuous improvements by letting them experience the benefits of them should be your goal. Without confining yourself to a framework for this meeting, generally called a *retrospective* in the Agile world, you should continually improve how you handle this meeting using lessons you learned from each past meeting.

## Summary

In this chapter, we discussed how to use VSTS/TFS effectively for post-iteration activities and for planning the next iteration. We evaluated some visualizing capabilities used to analyze the completed work in order to identify issues or any possible improvements.

In this chapter, we continued our focus on organizing and handling small and large teams, managing backlog, and working as Agile teams in iterations as well as post-iteration activities. In the next chapter, we look at some additional features you can utilize as a scrum master and that your team can utilize to help visualize and plan project roadmaps, facilitate business analysis, capture requirements, get stakeholder feedback, and provide visibility and accountability of the team activities.

# CHAPTER 5

# Roadmap/Project Plan and Resources

So far in this book, we have discussed how to use VSTS/TFS to manage different stages and issues that the team faces during software product/project development. In this chapter, we discuss planning the product roadmap or the project plan, facilitating the Business Analysis phase with office integration, and the mobile interface of VSTS/TFS. Also, we look at providing the visibility to top management by effectively utilizing the resources available within VSTS/TFS.

Whether you are working on a software project or product development, you and your team must have a plan that describes the path to completion. For project development, we normally use a project plan, and for software product development we use a product roadmap to illustrate when the project will be delivered or when the product features will be delivered. This chapter guides you on how to use various tools that you can integrated with VSTS/TFS to build such a plan.

In addition, we discuss how the business analysis functionality is facilitated with VSTS/TFS using the Microsoft Office integration and mobility. Also, we talk about how you can use all these resources to increase the visibility of the top management. Let's now dive deep into the facts.

© Chaminda Chandrasekara, Sanjaya Yapa 2018
C. Chandrasekara and S. Yapa, *Effective Team Management with VSTS and TFS*,
https://doi.org/10.1007/978-1-4842-3558-4_5

# Creating the Project Plan/Product Roadmap

As we discussed earlier in this book with Agile practices, the delivery timelines are tightly coupled to the iterations. That is, at the end of each iteration, or maybe every $x$ months, the team delivers goods to the end users. Program managers, project managers, or product owners are interested in visualizing when the artifacts are delivered to the end users. This level of information is crucial for the internal stakeholders so that they can keep the end users up to date with delivery timelines. Ideally, this information is illustrated in a plan so that both internal and external stakeholders can see the whereabouts of the development process. For a software project, as mentioned earlier, this takes the form of the project plan, and for product development, it is the product roadmap that showcases such information.

So here's the challenge: How do you create such a plan and keep the plan synchronized with ongoing work? There are many tools that you can used to create such a plan. The problem is that sometimes you have to manually update your plan based on the ongoing progress, or maybe the integration of such tools is very painful and time-consuming, or you have to spend time learning how to use new tools. VSTS/TFS has the answer to these challenges and also allows you to spending less time on learning and integration. Let's look at how you can use these integration tools effectively to create a nice, high-level picture that the stakeholders can use to see the project/product vision and the future.

## Creating the Project Plan/Product Roadmap

In earlier chapters, you learned how to create the backlog and set up the delivery cadence in VSTS/TFS. You can use the out-of-the-box Kanban boards for tracking daily progress with low-level details, but this does not give you an idea of the big picture that is relevant to the top-level managers and external stakeholders. However, one thing you can easily do is look at the Features backlog, and if the target dates are entered, you can get an idea of when the features will be delivered (Figure 5-1).

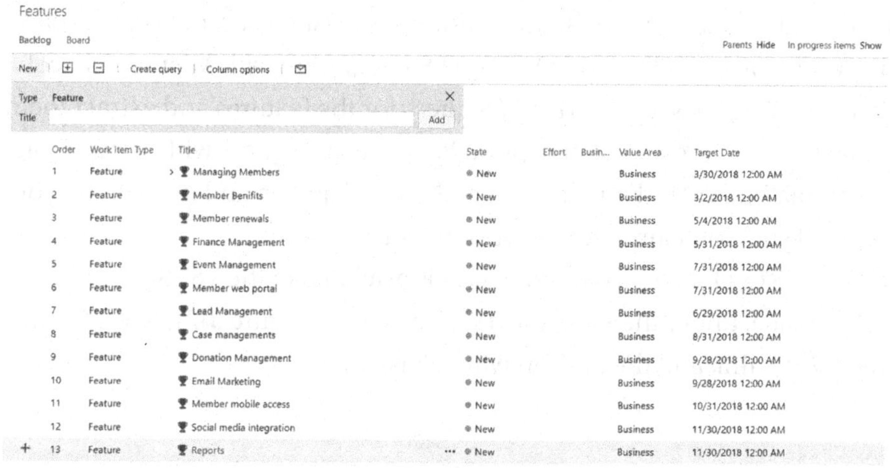

**Figure 5-1.** *Features with target dates*

This view gets pretty complex the more features you have because each feature is delivered in a different timeframe based on its business value and priority. Program managers, project managers, or product owners do not have time to go through every feature to build that one picture that illustrates the project plan/product roadmap, and you/your managers simply cannot present a list of features to the end users. As a workaround, you could write a query and extract features based on the timelines on which they will be delivered, or you could group the features using the query and have a separate list of features extracted to a given criteria. Neither of these techniques gives you or your superiors the expected level of information, however; it simply improves the clarity.

# Using Microsoft Excel

This is where Microsoft Office integration with VSTS/TFS becomes very handy without any cost. First, let's address the issue of preparing the road map or the project plan using VSTS/TFS integration with Microsoft Excel. First, you need to write a VSTS/TFS query for the features and extract them as a whole. The most obvious option is to open the query with Excel. From the Visual Studio Marketplace, select the Excel add-in and install it on your system if you don't already have it installed.

The VSTS Open in Excel extension is available in the VSTS Marketplace, under the Plan and Track category (Figure 5-2). Just click the green FREE link and the add-on will be installed.

***Figure 5-2.** Marketplace extensions*

When installed successfully, you can see an Excel icon within the query toolbar (Figure 5-3).

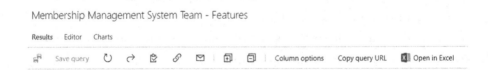

***Figure 5-3.** The Open in Excel extension*

To open your query with Excel, click the Team menu and then click New List to connect to VSTS/TFS with your credential. Then select the project and the list of queries is displayed. Figure 5-4 illustrates the query opened in Excel. Note that the results in Excel are automatically equipped with filters that you can use to filter out information. The best part of this is that you can use Excel features to manipulate the data you extract from VSTS/TFS.

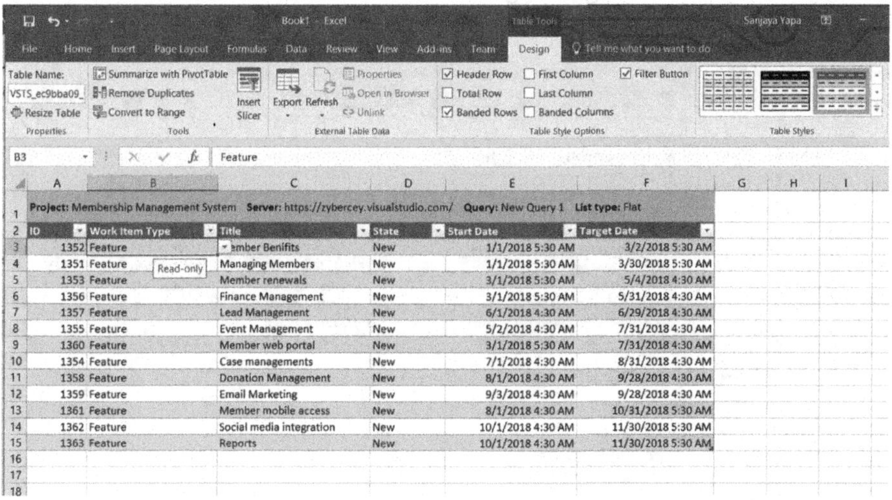

***Figure 5-4.*** *A query loaded in Excel*

As you can see, the query in Figure 5-4 extract features with target delivery timelines, which gives interested stakeholders a much better picture of what is going on. Because pretty much everyone knows how to use Excel, you can easily share information in this way with your end users. Basically, stakeholders are more interested in when the features are getting completed than the actual implementation details. But a view like the one in Figure 5-4 does not give them the information they want, especially when there are so many features in the backlog. This is common in large and complex projects/product development. Therefore in such scenarios, listing the features top to bottom may not be sufficient. They will still have to use the filters to see the relevant information, however.

By using the chart features in Excel, you can create a Gantt chart that illustrates the timelines (Figure 5-5). (Go to `https://www.ablebits.com/ office-addins-blog/2014/05/23/make-gantt-chart-excel/` to learn how to create this Gantt chart with Excel.) As you can see, this Gantt chart clearly shows the timelines and gives your stakeholders an idea of when the features are going to be available with just a quick glance. This appears to be a nice way of presenting some complex information. Basically, they do not have to scan throug a long list of features top to bottom.

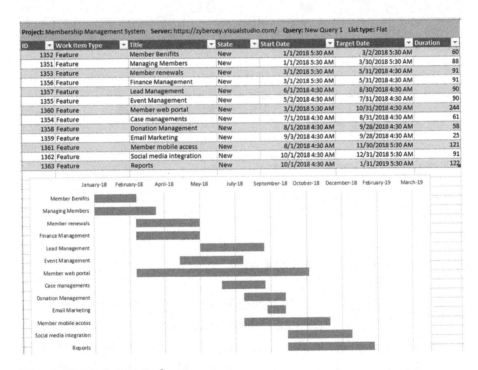

***Figure 5-5.***  *A Gantt chart*

There are some other templates you can use for similar purposes. In the next section, we look into integrating with Microsoft Project, which extends more capabilities and features.

# Integration with Microsoft Project

The project plan/product roadmap that we developed in the preceding scenario is kind of primitive. What if your stakeholders want to decide when to release the features based on client requests or based on the market demands? Or what if they want to see the resource allocation for each work item?

Microsoft Project is a great tool for handling such scenarios and it tracks ongoing work against time. Above all, it is popular among program managers, project managers, and product owners for tracking progress and identifying any delays. Whether you are working on a software product or project development, you can use Project to illustrate the project plan or the roadmap.

For this example, let's assume a scenario in which you have created the backlog with the help of your business analysts and now it is time for the stakeholders to decide when they want to see the features delivered. This is actually setting the high-level objectives for the team.

As the scrum master, your objective is to share the work items with the product owner/project or program managers so that they can decide when the items will be delivered to the end user. So how can you share the work items?

The steps are similar to the ones for using Excel:

1. First you must create a query to extract the required work items.

2. Then you need to open the results with Project by establishing a link between Project and VSTS/TFS.

3. To establish a connection between VSTS/TFS and Project, click the New List on Project's Ribbon. The Connect to Team Fondation Server window appears.

4. Select Team Foundation Server from the drop-down on the top or click the Server button to add a new connection.

5.  Finally, select the team project collection and
    then the appropriate team project. For further
    information, go to https://docs.microsoft.
    com/en-us/vsts/user-guide/connect-team-
    projects#connect-from-microsoft-excel-or-
    project.

With the latest release of Microsoft Project online, these capabilities
are extended and enhanced. On the Visual Studio Marketplace, you can
find more details (Figure 5-6).

***Figure 5-6.*** *Microsoft Project Marketplace extensions*

You can find more details on how to use Project here: https://docs.
microsoft.com/en-us/vsts/work/backlogs/office/create-your-
backlog-tasks-using-project.

One could argue that the stakeholders can't use VSTS/TFS to update
the timelines in our scenario. Of course they can, but only if they are
willing to open each and every feature and enter the starting and ending
timelines. The other problem with our scenario is, as we mentioned earlier,
it does not give stakeholders a high-level view from which to visualize the

timelines. Project gives this visualization, however. Figure 5-7 illustrates the results of the query we created to extract the features. As you can see, the start and finish dates are blank; your managers will decide when they want the releases to be available.

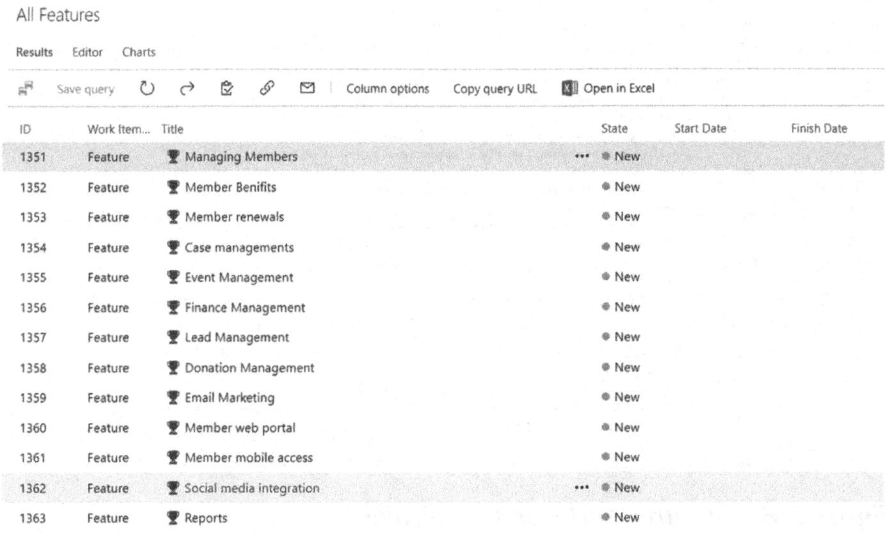

All Features

| | | | | | | |
|---|---|---|---|---|---|---|
| Results | Editor | Charts | | | | |

| ⊞ Save query | ↻ | ↷ | ⌂ | 𝒫 | ✉ | Column options | Copy query URL | ⊠ Open in Excel |

| ID | Work Item... | Title | State | Start Date | Finish Date |
|---|---|---|---|---|---|
| 1351 | Feature | 🏆 Managing Members | ••• ● New | | |
| 1352 | Feature | 🏆 Member Benifits | ● New | | |
| 1353 | Feature | 🏆 Member renewals | ● New | | |
| 1354 | Feature | 🏆 Case managements | ● New | | |
| 1355 | Feature | 🏆 Event Management | ● New | | |
| 1356 | Feature | 🏆 Finance Management | ● New | | |
| 1357 | Feature | 🏆 Lead Management | ● New | | |
| 1358 | Feature | 🏆 Donation Management | ● New | | |
| 1359 | Feature | 🏆 Email Marketing | ● New | | |
| 1360 | Feature | 🏆 Member web portal | ● New | | |
| 1361 | Feature | 🏆 Member mobile access | ● New | | |
| 1362 | Feature | 🏆 Social media integration | ••• ● New | | |
| 1363 | Feature | 🏆 Reports | ● New | | |

***Figure 5-7.*** *The feature backlog*

Figure 5-8 illustrate the query opened in Project. Note that it retrieves features as well as the user stories underneath them.

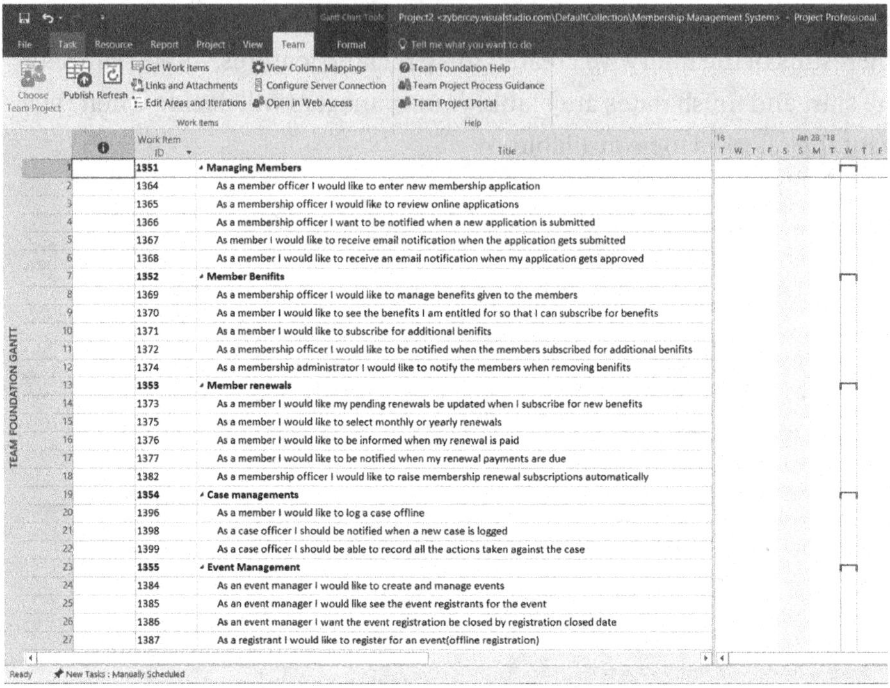

***Figure 5-8.*** *Features and stories in Project*

Now your managers can decide on and enter the dates for the items that will be delivered. Once this information is updated it can produce a Gantt Chart similar to the one in Figure 5-9. Stakeholders can even publish changes, which will update the VSTS/TFS work items as well.

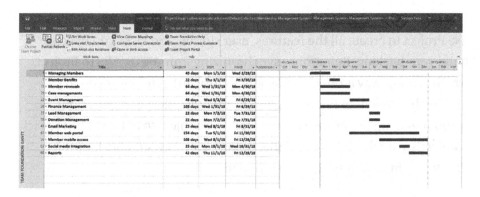

***Figure 5-9.*** *Gantt chart with Project*

Note that Project can connect and pass your updates to VSTS/TFS as soon you click the Publish button on the Ribbon; when you do, your backlog is updated (Figure 5-10). Project can be your top management window to the product/project backlog.

All Features

Results    Editor    Charts

Save query    ↻    ⇗    ⛶    🔗    ✉    |    Column options    Copy query URL    📗 Open in Excel

| ID | Work Item... | Title | State | Start Date | Finish Date |
|---|---|---|---|---|---|
| 1351 | Feature | 🏆 Managing Members | ••• ● New | 1/1/2018 2:30 AM | 2/28/2018 11:30 ... |
| 1352 | Feature | 🏆 Member Benifits | ● New | 3/1/2018 2:30 AM | 3/30/2018 11:30 ... |
| 1353 | Feature | 🏆 Member renewals | ● New | 1/31/2018 2:30 AM | 4/30/2018 12:30 ... |
| 1354 | Feature | 🏆 Case managements | ● New | 1/31/2018 2:30 AM | 4/30/2018 12:30 ... |
| 1355 | Feature | 🏆 Event Management | ● New | 5/2/2018 3:30 AM | 6/29/2018 12:30 ... |
| 1356 | Feature | 🏆 Finance Management | ● New | 1/31/2018 2:30 AM | 6/29/2018 12:30 ... |
| 1357 | Feature | 🏆 Lead Management | ● New | 7/2/2018 3:30 AM | 7/31/2018 12:30 ... |
| 1358 | Feature | 🏆 Donation Management | ● New | 7/2/2018 3:30 AM | 7/31/2018 12:30 ... |
| 1359 | Feature | 🏆 Email Marketing | ● New | 8/1/2018 3:30 AM | 8/31/2018 12:30 ... |
| 1360 | Feature | 🏆 Member web portal | ● New | 5/1/2018 3:30 AM | 11/30/2018 11:30... |
| 1361 | Feature | 🏆 Member mobile access | ● New | 8/1/2018 3:30 AM | 12/28/2018 11:30... |
| 1362 | Feature | 🏆 Social media integration | ••• ● New | 10/1/2018 3:30 AM | 10/31/2018 11:30... |
| 1363 | Feature | 🏆 Reports | ● New | 11/1/2018 2:30 AM | 12/28/2018 11:30... |

***Figure 5-10.*** *Dates updated in VSTS/TFS work items*

This is one particular scenario, but there are many times when you can use Project to create all the features, user stories, and tasks you need to build your backlog. Remember synchronizing from VSTS/TFS to Project, which is other way around, is not straightforward, it requires you to modify the work item templates and further technical configurations. So without making things too complicated, use Project to enhance VSTS/TFS connectivity and keep in mind that doing so is more suitable for project development than product development.

## Using Delivery Timelines

Now that we have looked into using Excel and Project to create project plans/product roadmap, you may be wondering what to do if your stakeholders want to see a more detailed view. Or let's say, for instance, that you have multiple teams working on a large project. In such scenarios, your stakeholders may want to know which team is working on what part of the project and when the features are going to be delivered. As we all now know, Project has features to manage resources, but these are two different tools and you and your stakeholder have to shift between the tools to access information. This will be cumbersome when there are multiple teams working in a large complex project. This means that you are not using VSTS/TFS to its full potential for creating a better plan. You could integrate on-premises TFS with the Project server, as explained in https://docs.microsoft.com/en-us/vsts/work/tfs-ps-sync/ synchronize-tfs-project-server, but this is no longer supported in TFS 2017 and newer.

So, by utilizing VSTS/TFS, you can create a nice delivery plan for your stakeholders by simply installing the Delivery Plans add-on from the Plan and Track category of the VSTS Marketplace (Figure 5-11). Just click the green FREE link underneath the title and the add-on will be installed.

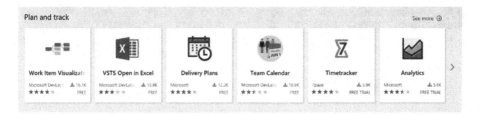

***Figure 5-11.*** *The Delivery Plans extension*

Once you install the Delivery Plans add-on, you can see a Plan tab right next to the Backlog and Queries tabs. So, where exactly can we use this tool and what level of information does it give us? Sometimes two or more teams will be working together on the same project, probably either because of the complexity or to speed up the delivery. Your program manager/product owner wants to see this whole picture.

You can easily put up a delivery plan. No queries are required, and you can use the existing information from the backlog. Remember, for the tool to work, you must first set up the teams and your release cadence. Also, you must assign your work items to the teams. Once you have done this, it is easy to build the delivery plan. Just click the New button to create a new plan and in the New Delivery Plan window, provide the Plan Name, Project, Team, and the Backlog. Once the plan is created, you can see it listed as illustrated in Figure 5-12.

***Figure 5-12.*** *Delivery plans*

The nice thing about this add-on is that you can have multiple plans, which make it an ideal tool for product management. Usually, for product management, you need to have a current plan and a future plan in which the future plan provides information to answer end user queries.

So, let's move back to our scenario in which multiple teams are working on the same project. When you set up your plan, it will look something like Figure 5-13.

At the top, this plan highlights when the features will be delivered, and in order to deliver the features, what user stories must be complete and when. You can easily move the work items and define the release timelines; for instance, in this case, every two months there will be a release. Figure 5-14 illustrates a similar scenario.

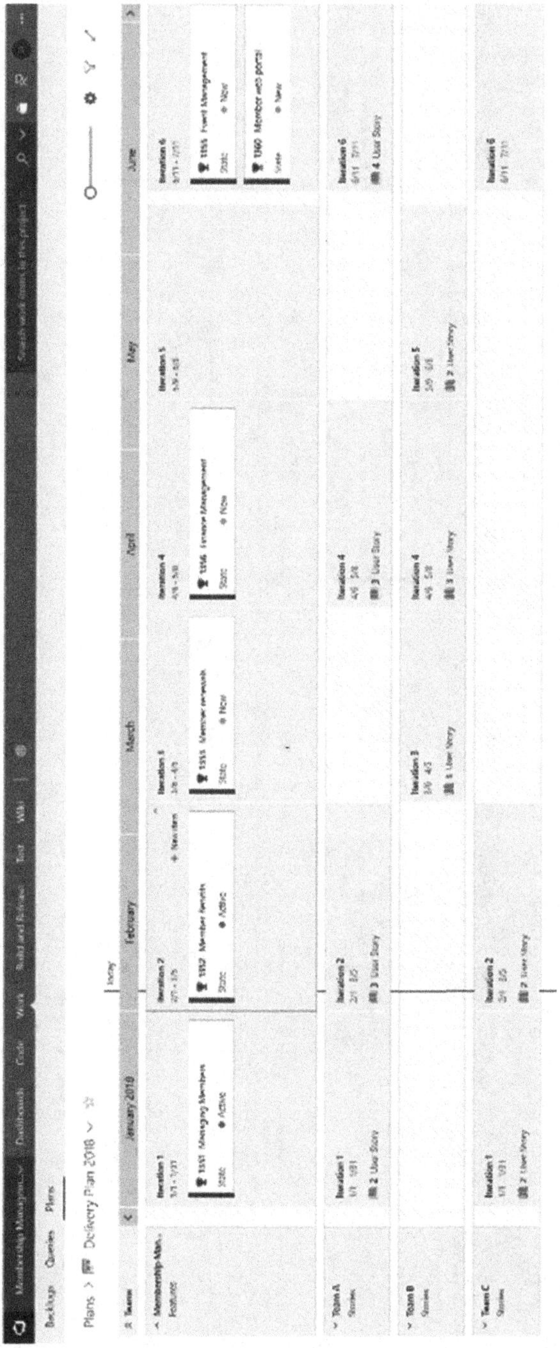

*Figure 5-13. A delivery plan*

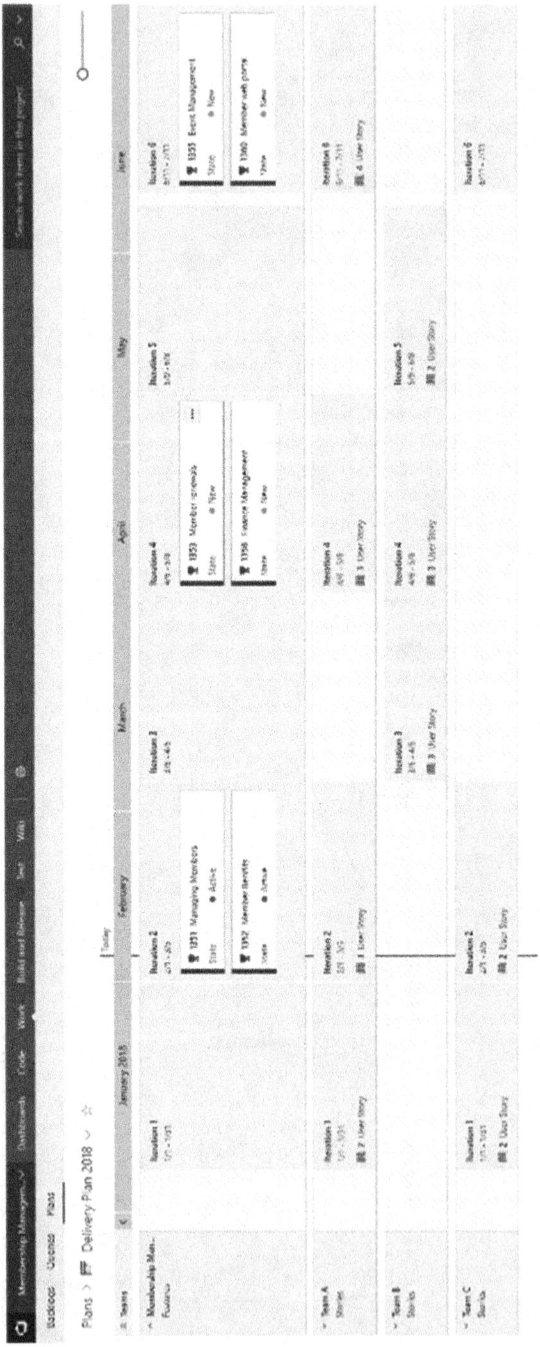

*Figure 5-14. Another delivery plan*

For more information on delivery plans, refer to `https://docs.microsoft.com/en-us/vsts/work/scale/review-team-plans`.

## Power BI Integration

For progress reporting, Microsoft Power BI is the number one tool available, and it has some exceptional reporting capabilities. While executing a project, you are required to report the progress you are making and how well the project is doing. In addition to built-in VSTS/TFS dashboards, you can use Power BI integration to build state-of-the-art dashboards for VSTS. (As of the time of the writing of this book, Power BI integratation is supported in VSTS only. TFS on-premise support will be added in a future TFS version). You can find the Open In Power BI plugin in the VSTS Marketplace under the Plan and Track category (Figure 5-15). In addition to this extension, there are few dependencies. For instance, there are three data connection mechanisms and prerequisites which are listed in detail in the URI provided below.

***Figure 5-15.*** *The Open in Power BI marketplace extension*

Once it is installed successfully, you can see the Open in Power BI links, as illustrated in Figure 5-16.

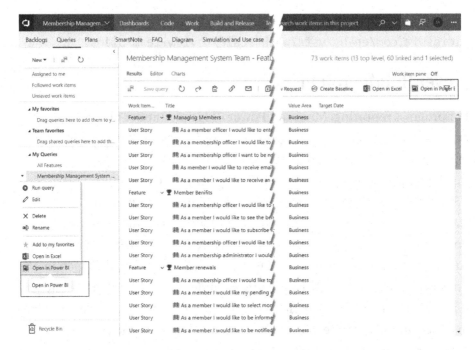

**Figure 5-16.** *The Open in Power BI links*

Remember you must have Power BI installed on your computer, and you should also check out the other dependencies, described at https://docs.microsoft.com/en-us/vsts/report/powerbi/overview, like the Analytics extension, which we discussed in Chapter 4. When you click these options, the work items of the query are downloaded as .pbit files. You can open these via the Power BI desktop application, and to do so, you need to provide credentials. Once you have opened a work item, you have access to the rich features to create a nice Power BI dashboard (Figure 5-17).

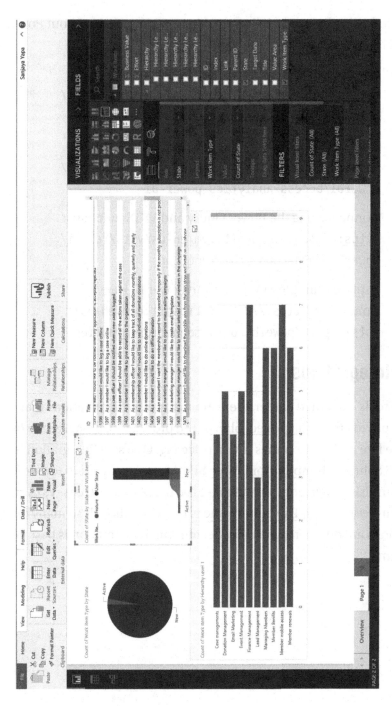

*Figure 5-17. The Power BI dashboard*

The following links may help you gain more knowledge about Power BI/VSTS integration.

- Connect to VSTS with the Power BI Date Connector: https://docs.microsoft.com/en-us/vsts/report/powerbi/data-connector-connect

- Connect to VSTS using the Power BI ODate feed: https://docs.microsoft.com/en-us/vsts/report/powerbi/access-analytics-power-bi

- Connect using the Power Query and VSTS functions: https://docs.microsoft.com/en-us/vsts/report/powerbi/data-connector-functions

- Explore example reports for the Power BI Data Connector: https://docs.microsoft.com/en-us/vsts/report/powerbi/data-connector-examples

## Other Integrations

Like the tools explained earlier, there are many other integrations that you can use to create the project plan or the product roadmap. Some of them are free and some comes with a price tag. One such integration is the VSTS Solution Template for Power BI (https://powerbi.microsoft.com/en-us/blog/announcing-visual-studio-team-services-vsts-solution-template/). The bottom line is that even though so many fancy integrations are out there, you must decide which integration is best for your team.

# Business Analysis

As we all know, business analysis is one of the tedious activities in a project lifecycle. Either business analysts or product owners must take over this task, and it is one of the important activities as requirement clarity has an immense impact on the success of a project. Instinctively, these two groups are likely to use Microsoft Word to capture the requirements in the form of a requirements document. Later they will enter the requirements into the project/product management tool used by your team. Needless to say, this doubles the effort needed and requires more time.

This task gets even harder when changes are coming in from the end users before the sign-up. Now the business analyst/product owner must update both the document and the content in your tool. The problem becomes worse if the scale of the project is bigger and changes will have critical impacts. In this section, we discuss the answer to these problems with more familiar tools such as Microsoft Office integrated with VSTS/TFS.

# Office Integration

Traditionally, business analysts or product owners have written the requirements as a document, the *requirements documentation*. But the development team works with a tool to manage work items such as VSTS/TFS and conventionally, developers do not like to read lengthy documents. So, either you, the scrum master, or the business analyst or product owner must convert and enter the requirements into the VSTS/TFS, which requires additional effort and time.

We all use Microsoft Office for documentation purposes. Microsoft Word, PowerPoint, and Visio are key tools required for business analysis activities. The good news is that to overcome the issues just mentioned, you don't have to learn new tools. It is just a matter of using the tools that you are familiar with together with VSTS/TFS and reducing the workload.

# Smart Office4TFS

This third-party tool, available at (`www.modernrequirements.com/ product/smartoffice4tfs-professional-2/`), is popular among modern business analysts and directly addresses the issues just mentioned. It also creates a more collaborative platform on which, from the beginning, all of your team members can stay up to date with ongoing work. This tool integrates with Microsoft Word, Visio, Outlook, and Excel. First, let's discuss how this tool can help you create requirements.

Let's assume that your business analyst/product owner has been commissioned to write the requirements for a project; the process of identifying and documenting requirements is tedious but vital. If the requirements are not captured correctly, then the end result will not meet user expectations. This is not a state that any of us want to be in. Therefore, to capture the user requirements accurately, the business analyst or the product owner has to continue discussions with the end users during the requirements capturing phase. Remember, no matter how many sessions you participate in to capture the requirements, they will change. As Agile teams, we accept this fact.

Imagine you are discussing the high-level business flows with the client, and at the same time, you are using Visio to create the process flow. Changing this time and again until you finalize the flow with the client is going to be a painful task. But Smart Visio4Tfs (`https://marketplace. visualstudio.com/items?itemName=ModernRequirementsbyeDevTe ch.SmartVisio4TFS`) will save the day for you by allowing you to create the feature in TFS as soon as you create the flow diagram. You can easily publish the changes back to VSTS/TFS by just clicking the Publish button.

And this is not it! For each stage of the process flow, you can create the user stories and relevant tasks directly from Visio. The same applies to Smart Word4TFS (`https://marketplace.visualstudio.com/ items?itemName=edevtech-mr.SmartOffice4TFS`), where you can use the predefined templates for the Agile, Scrum, or CMMI process templates to define the work items. These templates can map the work item hierarchy of your process template.

Additionally, you can use Smart Outlook4TFS to perform the tasks related to requirements capture. Also, through Outlook, you can easily manage your backlog.

Smart Excel4TFS is capable of automatically generating various matrixes, such as such as the Requirements Traceability matrix, Work Item Decomposition matrixes, and so on. This is especially useful in scenarios in which exceptionally large volumes of work items exist in your project, the SmartExcel4TFS allow you to visualize the relationship between the work items. This setup also allows you to organize the work items in different perspectives, which is useful in product management and program management.

## Using PowerPoint for Storyboarding

When we are capturing business requirements, presenting the requirements as a wireframe helps illustrate our understanding of the requirements. You can use so many tools to create the wireframes that are available in the market, but keeping them synchronized with your requirements is a challenge. The top benefits of creating wireframes are that they increase the user's level of understanding and improve the user's experience. On the other hand, one picture is worth a thousand words.

Out of the box, TFS/VSTS integrates with Microsoft PowerPoint, which enables you to create amazing wireframes. Just click the wireframe link on the drop-down of the work item and you can create a wireframe to represent your requirements. Figure 5-18 illustrates how to start a storyboard for a user story.

***Figure 5-18.*** *Starting storyboarding for a user story*

When you are directed to PowerPoint, find the Storyboarding tab on the Ribbon to open the storyboarding tools (Figure 5-19).

***Figure 5-19.*** *Storyboarding tools*

You can use these tools to build up the wireframes for your requirements (Figure 5-20).

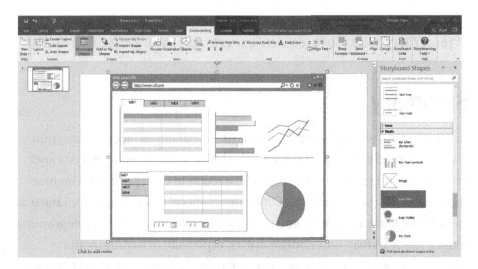

***Figure 5-20.*** *Storyboarding with PowerPoint*

Again, when you use this method, you don't have to learn any new
tools and you use a tool that you already familiar with. You can learn more
about the storyboarding here: `https://docs.microsoft.com/en-us/vsts/`
`work/backlogs/office/storyboard-your-ideas-using-powerpoint`.

One important thing to keep in mind is that you might not need all
these integrations. So think carefully and chose the tools that you need to
improve the productivity of the team as a whole.

# The Mobile Interface

At present, mobile access to any application is essential, especially when
we are working at client sites gathering requirements and attending
workshops. It would be ideal if you could enter requirements into the
backlog directly from your tablet while you are discussing them with
your client. To address this, Microsoft has started to improve the mobile
interface of VSTS/TFS. At the time of the writing this book, mobile
access to the application is very primitive, but the good news is that it is
continuously improving.

You can find more information about the mobile interface here:
`https://docs.microsoft.com/en-us/vsts/collaborate/mobile-work`.

# Summary

In this chapter, we discussed several issues/challenges faced by program managers, product owners, project managers, and business analysts and how various integrations of TFS can be used to overcome them. The nice thing about all these Microsoft Office integrations is that you do not have to spend time learning new tools or practices. Additionally, these integrations reduce the workload and remove errors, especially in requirements capture. As a scrum master, you can use these Office integrations together with your top managers and direct the team to success in delivering the end-user expectations.

In the next chapter, we look at options for customizing VSTS/TFS to adopt to your team's process, rather than your team adapting to the tool.

# CHAPTER 6

# Adapting VSTS/TFS to Your Team's Process

In Chapters 1 through 4, we looked at how to run Agile development while leveraging the capabilities VSTS/TFS has to offer. Then in Chapter 5, we discussed project roadmaps and project plans and how to integrate Microsoft Office with VSTS/TFS to understand how VSTS/TFS can help you get a holistic view of a project/product.

We also talked about how you should not adapt to the tool demands; instead, you should adapt the tool to a process that works better for your team. As your team continually improves the process, the tool should be able to adapt accordingly. In this chapter, we explore the capabilities of VSTS/TFS from the perspective of adaptability to your process. Customizability in VSTS/TFS can be identified in following broader categories.

- Customizing shared resources

- Customizing team projects and processes

- Customizing access to work tracking tools

- Customizing the test experience

- Additional customization options

© Chaminda Chandrasekara, Sanjaya Yapa 2018
C. Chandrasekara and S. Yapa, *Effective Team Management with VSTS and TFS*,
https://doi.org/10.1007/978-1-4842-3558-4_6

VSTS and on-premises TFS have different customization capabilities; we discuss them in detail under each of the broad categories we cover in this chapter. You can adapt VSTS/TFS to your team's needs with this knowledge.

In addition to customizations, we look at the pros and cons of using VSTS (cloud) vs. TFS (on-premises) for your team needs.

# Customizing Shared Resources

Area paths, iteration paths, tags, and shared queries are few important shared resources that you can customize. Area paths allow you to group work items by product, feature, or team area. Iteration paths allow you to group work into time-related events, such as iterations/sprints or milestones. Tags let you filter your backlog items in queries. You can use shared queries to obtain information on work items and visualize them using query-based charts and dashboards that include those charts, which can be shared among the team. Additionally, you can create private queries only visible to you. We discussed these items and how to use them effectively in previous chapters.

# Customizing Team Projects and Processes

Customizing the team project and process allows you to change VSTS/TFS to adapt to the process of your team. VSTS/TFS contains three types of process templates.

- Agile

- Scrum

- CMMI

Three major types of process customizations are available in VSTS/TFS depending on whether you are using the cloud or on-premise instances and based on how the VSTS (cloud) instance is created.

- *Inheritance:* This customization is only available in VSTS and it supports WYSIWIG (what-you-see-is-what-you-get) editing.

- *Hosted XML:* This customization is only available in VSTS accounts migrated from on-premises TFS. Customizations are possible via the export and import of process templates.

- *On-premises XML:* This customization is only available for on-premises TFS, and customizations are possible via the export and import of process templates.

# Customizing VSTS with Template Inheritance

VSTS allows you to inherit the default available Agile, Scrum, or CMMI templates to customize them. You are not normally allowed to customize the system/default template; in order to do so, you must create an inherited template. Once you've created this template, you can introduce new fields, hide existing fields, change the status workflow of work items, introduce new work items, and so on. You can create an inherited process template using the existing default template in the Process tab of the VSTS Account Admin mode as shown in Figure 6-1.

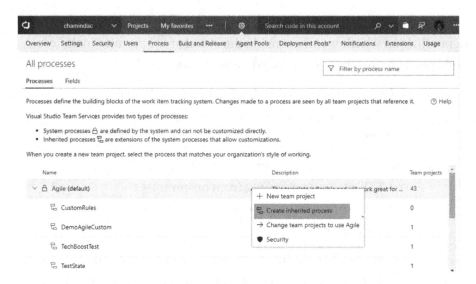

***Figure 6-1.*** *Creating an inherited process template*

Once you have created an inherited template, you can change the existing team project to use it or you can create a new team project with the inherited template. The changes you make in an inherited template are applied to all projects that use that template. In following sections, we discuss a few scenarios you may want to customize. You can use the Witadmin command-line tool in VSTS accounts with the inheritance process model to list information about team projects (`https://docs.microsoft.com/en-us/vsts/work/customize/reference/witadmin/witadmin-customize-and-manage-objects-for-tracking-work`).

# Adding a Custom Field

You have the option of setting up new fields with different input types; for example, you may create a field that expects text data or numeric data or a text-based pick list or a numeric picklist (Figure 6-2). If you require a checkbox type of a field, you can set its Type as a Boolean field. The Identity field type allows you to define fields similar to the Assign To field in a work item. If you have synced with Azure Active Directory (AAD), this field lists the users in your active directory in the custom field, which is similar to the Assigned To field. This type of field is useful for defining a supervisor, or a Report To user, for the user who is assigned the particular work item.

*Figure 6-2.* *Adding a custom field*

You can make a custom field mandatory for a given work item and make it nonmandatory for another work item by checking or unchecking the Required option as shown in Figure 6-3. Additionally, it is possible to set a default value for a field. By editing the existing system fields in a given work item, you can also make them mandatory or not.

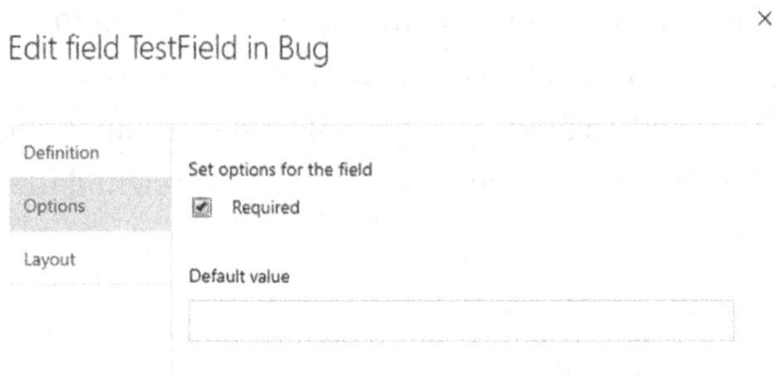

Edit field TestField in Bug                                    ×

Definition

Options          Set options for the field
                 ☑  Required

Layout
                 Default value

*Figure 6-3.*  *Making a filed mandatory for a work item*

You can place an added custom field in any of the available layout
groups, such as Classification, Planning, and so on, or you can create a
new layout group and place the new custom field in it. It is also possible
to edit the layout group of the custom field after you created it, but it is not
possible to change an existing default field layout group (Figure 6-4).

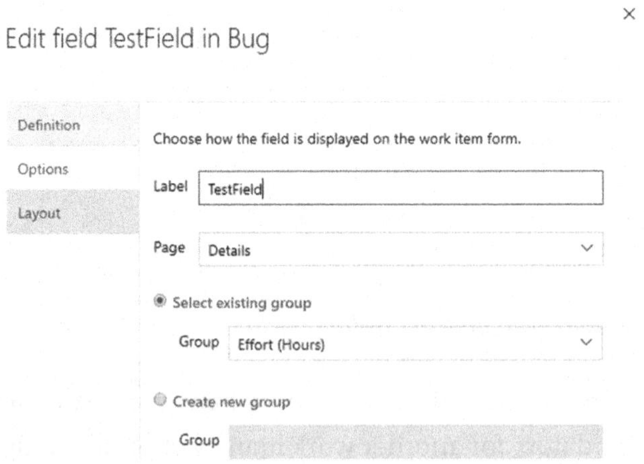

Edit field TestField in Bug                                    ×

Definition
                 Choose how the field is displayed on the work item form.

Options          Label  | TestField |

Layout
                 Page   | Details                               ∨ |

                 ◉ Select existing group

                 Group  | Effort (Hours)                        ∨ |

                 ○ Create new group

                 Group

*Figure 6-4.*  *Defining a layout group for a custom field*

You can find more information on custom fields for work items at
`https://docs.microsoft.com/en-us/vsts/work/customize/process/`
`customize-process-field?toc=/vsts/work/customize/toc.json&bc=/`
`vsts/work/customize/breadcrumb/toc.json#add-a-custom-field`.

## Modifying an Existing Field

You may want to alter an existing field or change selectable value options.
But be aware that the only allowed changes for an existing field are
changing a default value, making the field mandatory or not, or changing
its label. If you want to make more modifications to a field, you can hide
the existing field (Figure 6-5) and add a custom field with the same label.

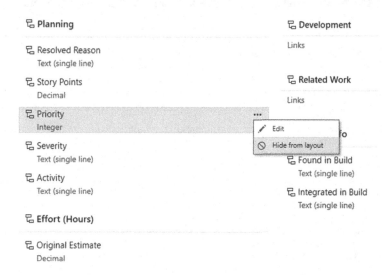

***Figure 6-5.***  *Hiding an existing field*

# Changing the Status Workflow of a Work Item

If you do not like the columns in the work item boards, refer back to Chapter 2, where we discussed how to add new columns or change existing columns. But in that discussion, you were limited to the available set of state values in the work item and you may have used the same state in multiple columns of the board for a work item. With inherited process templates, you can now define your own states for a work item. You can use a new custom state that you define in a work item in another work item as well. You also have the option of hiding existing states (Figure 6-6) in a work item so that you can create your own custom state workflow.

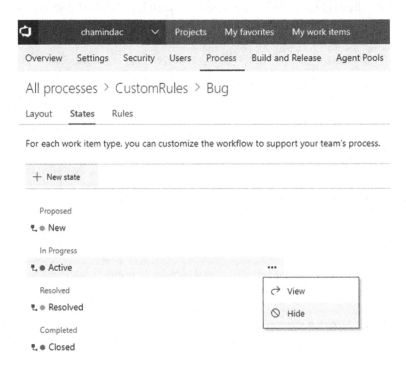

***Figure 6-6.*** *Add a new state or hide an existing state*

However, you cannot hide a state if it is the only state in a given state category, such as Proposed, InProgress, and so on. You are not allowed to add new state categories except the categories that are available by default. Another limitation is that you cannot add a new state or hide an existing state in the Completed category at the time of the writing of this book. However, you may add a state to an available but by default unused state category in a given work item template. For example, the Removed state category is not used in the Agile template bug work item by default, but you can introduce a new state to this category in the bug work item using an inherited template.

Once you set up the new states in your work items, you may have to alter the board columns in the Work tab (`https://docs.microsoft.com/ en-us/vsts/work/kanban/add-columns#add-or-rename-columns`) to reflect the changes and the board may not be viewable until you fix the board columns with visible states if you have hidden any existing states from a work item.

## Custom Rules

You may want to add your own rules to work items depending on the field values or state changes in a work item. For example, you can set a rule so that a product backlog item cannot move to the InProgress state from a Proposed state if the work item's Acceptance Criteria (Definition of Done) is not defined. Custom rules enable you to enforce the process steps (Figure 6-7).

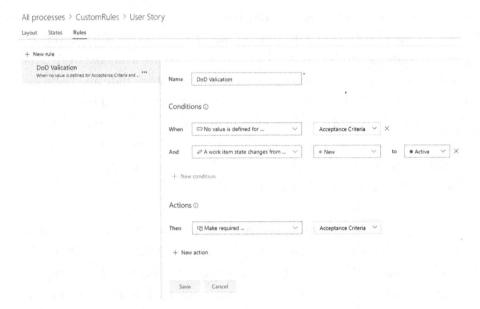

*Figure 6-7.* *Defining custom rules*

## Custom Backlog Levels and Work Items

If you find available portfolio backlog levels are not sufficient for your team's needs, you can add additional top levels to the portfolio backlog as shown in Figure 6-8. You can define a new work item type and assign it to the new level.

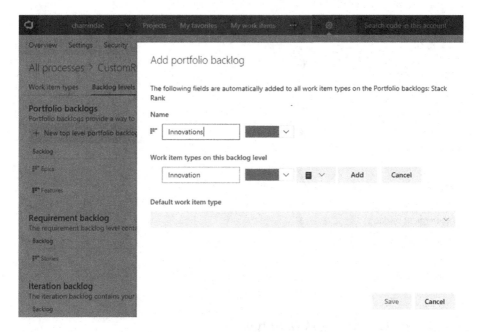

***Figure 6-8.*** *Adding a new portfolio backlog level*

You can add any additional work item types to any backlog level as you require (Figure 6-9). You can set the default work item type for the backlog level and even select a new custom work item as the default work item for the backlog level.

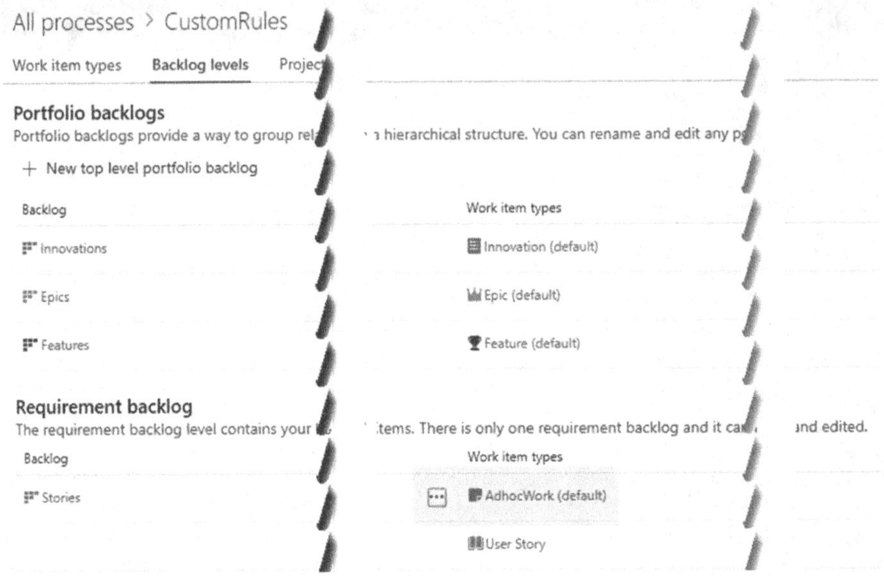

All processes > CustomRules

Work item types    **Backlog levels**    Proje

**Portfolio backlogs**
Portfolio backlogs provide a way to group rel⌐          ⌐ hierarchical structure. You can rename and edit any p⌐

+ New top level portfolio backlog

Backlog                                                    Work item types

🏳 Innovations                                             ▦ Innovation (default)

🏳 Epics                                                   ⅢⅡ Epic (default)

🏳 Features                                                🏆 Feature (default)

**Requirement backlog**
The requirement backlog level contains your ⌐     ⌐ :tems. There is only one requirement backlog and it ca⌐ .     ⌐nd edited.

Backlog                                                   Work item types

🏳 Stories                              [···]   🏳 AdhocWork (default)

                                                ⅢⅡ User Story

*Figure 6-9.*  *Custom work item types*

# Customizing VSTS with Hosted XML

Hosted XML is available only in VSTS when you have migrated an on-premises TFS project collection to VSTS (`https://docs.microsoft.com/en-us/vsts/articles/migrate-to-vsts-from-tfs`). In a migrated VSTS account, default process templates and process templates with customizations from projects that are migrated are available. You can export any of the default or project-based custom templates, modify them, and import them, overwriting a project-based custom template in the process. You are allowed to export a default template and import it as a custom template, but you cannot import a process template with a default template name, meaning you cannot overwrite default templates. Instead, you can create a new project with the default or custom process templates. Ignore the warning in Figure 6-10, as this image was taken from a dry run migration of TFS to VSTS.

Overview   Settings   Security   Users   Process   Build and Release   Agent Pools   Deployment Pools*   Notifications   Extensions   Usage

⚠ VS403262: This dry run account will expire and be deleted shortly after or on 2/27/2018. To continue testing beyond this date you will need to repeat the dry run import.

## All processes

▽ Filter by process name

Processes   Fields

Processes define the building blocks of the work item tracking system. Changes made to a process are seen by all team projects that reference it.    ⑦ Help

Visual Studio Team Services provides two types of processes:

- System processes 🔒 are defined by the system and can not be customized directly.
- Inherited processes 🗗 are extensions of the system processes that allow customizations.

When you create a new team project, select the process that matches your organization's style of working.

+ Import process

| Name | Description | Team projects |
|------|-------------|---------------|
| 🔒 Agile (default) | This template is flexible and will work great for most te... | 0 |
| 🔒 Scrum | This template is for teams who follow the Scrum frame... | 0 |
| 🔒 CMMI | This template is for more formal projects requiring a fr... | 0 |
| ⟨⟩ | This process was exported from a project but no descri... | 1 |
| ⟨⟩ | This process was exported from a project but no descri... | 1 |
| ⟨⟩ | ed from a project but no descri... | 1 |
| ⟨⟩ | ed from a project but no descri... | 1 |
| ⟨⟩ | ed from a project but no descri... | 1 |

··· 
+ New team project
Set as default process
Disable process
↩ Export

*Figure 6-10.* *Exporting a process template*

It is possible to create an inherited process template from the default process templates when you are using a TFS-to-VSTS–migrated account (Figure 6-11). More information on Hosted XML–based template customizations can be found at `https://docs.microsoft.com/en-us/vsts/work/customize/import-process/customize-process`.

Overview   Settings   Security   Users   Process   Build and Release   Agent Pools   Deployment Pools*   Notifications   Extensions   Usage

⚠ VS403262: This dry run account will expire and be deleted shortly after or on 2/27/2018. To continue testing beyond this date you will need to repeat the dry run import.

## All processes

Processes   Fields

Processes define the building blocks of the work item tracking system. Changes made to a process are seen by all team projects that reference it.        ⑦ Help

Visual Studio Team Services provides two types of processes:

• System processes 🔒 are defined by the system and can not be customized directly.
• Inherited processes 🗏 are extensions of the system processes that allow customizations.

When you create a new team project, select the process that matches your organization's style of working.

+ Import process

| Name | Description | Team projects |
| --- | --- | --- |
| 🔒 Agile (default) | This template is flexible and will work great for most te... | 0 |
| 🔒 Scrum | ow the Scrum frame... | 0 |
| 🔒 CMMI | ojects requiring a fr... | 0 |
| </> | ⋅roject but no descri... | 1 |

··· 
+ New team project
🗏 Create inherited process
→ Change team projects to use Agile
↩ Export
🛡 Security

*Figure 6-11.* *Inheriting and exporting is supported in the default process template*

You can use the Witadmin command-line tool in VSTS accounts with the Hosted XML process model to list information about team projects (https://docs.microsoft.com/en-us/vsts/work/customize/reference/witadmin/witadmin-customize-and-manage-objects-for-tracking-work).

# Customizing with TFS On-premises XML

The most customizable process template type is on-premises XML, which is only available for TFS (Figure 6-12). This process template type is similar to Hosted XML; using it, you can export a custom template or a default template, but you are only allowed to import as a custom template. However, you cannot create inherited templates from default templates in on-premises XML, so there is no WYSIWIG editing available for TFS at the time of the writing of this book. More information on on-premises XML process model customizations can be found at https://docs.microsoft.com/en-us/vsts/work/customize/on-premises-xml-process-model.

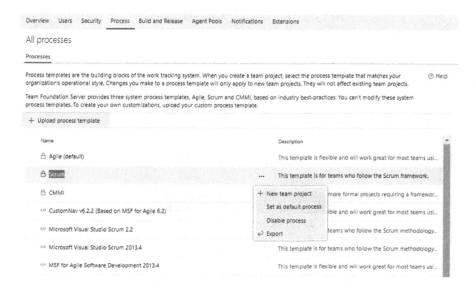

*Figure 6-12.* *Options for on-premises XML*

The Witadmin command-line tool can be used for listing as well as editing the template in on-premises XML (https://docs.microsoft. com/en-us/vsts/work/customize/reference/witadmin/witadmin-customize-and-manage-objects-for-tracking-work).

# Customizing the Access to Work Tracking Tools

In VSTS/TFS there are many options that restrict or grant users access to different features or work tracking items. When you add a member to a team in a team project, by default, the contributor access permissions are granted to that user, enabling the user to contribute most of the work to code, builds and deployments, work items, and testing. Refer to https://docs. microsoft.com/en-us/vsts/security/permissions-access to understand the general permission and access control settings in VSTS and TFS. More information is available at https://docs.microsoft.com/en-us/vsts/ security/about-permissions, and subtopics appear under How-To Guides highlighted in the Figure 6-13.

***Figure 6-13.*** *Permissions topics*

# Customizing the Test Experience

Testing is an important aspect of the software delivery process as we have discussed in previous chapters. How to customize the testing experience for different configurations is explained at `https://docs.microsoft.com/en-us/vsts/manual-test/test-different-configurations`.

# Additional Customization Options

If you find that the level of customization to VSTS/TFS as explained in the preceding sections is not sufficient for your process needs, you can move on to these unsupported, but often used, customization options:

- As we have discussed several times in this book, you can use Visual Studio Marketplace tools (`https://marketplace.visualstudio.com/vsts`) to add additional behavior changes to your VSTS/TFS.

- You can create your own tools and add them to your VSTS/TFS. To create the tools you need, use the extension project template information at `https://marketplace.visualstudio.com/items?itemName=JoshGarverick.VSTSExtensionProjectTemplates`. When creating your own tools, you are able to utilize REST API for VSTS/TFS (`https://docs.microsoft.com/en-us/rest/api/vsts/`). The extensions you create can be published to Visual Studio Marketplace for others to use (`https://docs.microsoft.com/en-us/vsts/extend/publish/overview`).

- If you do not find the feature you want and you are unable to create your own tool, then you can opt to request that feature from Microsoft here: `https://visualstudio.uservoice.com/forums/330519-team-services`.

# The Pros and Cons of VSTS vs. TFS

The major benefits of using VSTS over TFS are that you do not have to manage the infrastructure needs of TFS and you get feature updates automatically, every three weeks. Normally you get quarterly updates for on-premises TFS, but performing those upgrades is your responsibility—they do not happen automatically.

You also have to perform upgrades to on-premises TFS when new versions are released, and doing so may require you to upgrade your servers' operating systems, their SQL server version, and so on, as per the requirement of the released TFS version.

However, for VSTS, in order to build your projects, you may need to maintain your own build infrastructure with agents (`https://docs.microsoft.com/en-us/vsts/build-release/actions/agents/v2-windows`, `https://docs.microsoft.com/en-us/vsts/build-release/actions/agents/v2-osx`, `https://docs.microsoft.com/en-us/vsts/build-release/actions/agents/v2-linux`) configured on your own hardware if your team has a specific SDK or other software needs that are not available in the hosted build services (`https://docs.microsoft.com/en-us/vsts/build-release/concepts/agents/hosted`).

You have greater customization ability in on-premise TFS than in VSTS, but in VSTS, WYSIWIG editing in the inheritance process model is more appealing than the XML customizations.

VSTS comes with a monthly recurring cost and TFS has a different pricing model. More details on VSTS/TFS pricing can be found at `https://docs.microsoft.com/en-us/vsts/billing/`.

# Summary

In this chapter, we looked at the various customization options that are available in VSTS/TFS to enable you to adapt the tool to suite your process needs. It is important for you to remember that the tool is not what is improving how your teams perform, it is the process that is continually improved by the team that utilizes the tool and adapts the tool to the needs of the team making successful project/product deliveries a possibility.

In this book, we have gone through how you as a scrum master should utilize VSTS/TFS as a tool to support your teams process improvements. In the first four chapters, we discussed various aspects of VSTS/TFS including handling Agile projects, managing backlogs, planning iterations, working within a day, and how to work after an iteration. In the final two chapters, we discussed roadmaps and planning and the customization capabilities that are available in VSTS/TFS to adapt the tool to the team's needs.

# Index

## A

Application lifecycle management
 (ALM) tool, 1

## B

Backlog
 bug management options, 36
 defects/bugs, 35
 grooming sessions, 32, 37
  acceptance criteria, 39
  area, 40
  description, 40
  DoD, 37–38
  DoR-met backlog items, 38
  estimation, 42
  iteration, 40
  prioritization, 40, 42
  story points/effort/size, 39
  stakeholder feedback, 45
  title, 39
  test and feedback browser, 45
  velocity chart, 44
  work item fields, 39
 iteration, 96
 large team planning, 55

levels of, 32
Kanban boards, 46–50
small team planning
 advantages, 51
 capacity planning, 53–54
 Dev team, 50
 story point burndown, 52
 task estimations, 51–53
sprint zero/no-sprint/
 pre-sprint, 56
visualization, 55
work definition
 categories, 30
 delivers value, 30–31
 requirements, 30
 spike items, 31–32
 support work, 31
 user stories, 30

## C

Cumulative flow diagram (CFD)
 bulges, 108
 chart, 106–107
 flat lines and scope
  changes, 109
 work in progress, 107

## W, X, Y, Z

Printed in the United States
By Bookmasters